# BE SURE YOUR MESSAGE GETS TO THE BUYER

BY

## HERMAN R. WILLIAMS

Effective Marketing Tools for the
Professional in Real Estate

PAGE PUBLISHING, INC.
Conneaut Lake, PA

First originally published by Page Publishing 2022

ISBN 978-1-6624-7355-5 (pbk)
ISBN 978-1-6624-7356-2 (digital)

Printed in the United States of America

# CONTENTS

## PART TWO
## HOW TO DO A FEASIBILITY STUDY
## FOR A PROSPECTIVE INVESTOR

## COMMERCIAL REAL ESTATE
## SESSION No. 3
## *THE SHOPPING CENTER*

### PART 1

### PART 2

## FEASIBILITY OF PROPOSED COMMERCIAL REAL ESTATE
## SESSION No. ONE
## THE OFFICE BUILDING

## COMMERCIAL REAL ESTATE
## SESSION No. TWO
## THE OFFICE BUILDING

## Section Three
## FOREIGN INVESTORS IN UNITED STATES REAL ESTATE

## Additional Taxes Imposed on Foreign Corporations Having Branch in United States

# BE SURE YOUR MESSAGE
# GETS TO THE BUYER

This guidebook concerns the most important investment you will ever make in the operation of your business—advertising.

We strongly urge you to have your sales staff read it, particularly those who write their own ad-copy. Advertising is the "keystone" in the art of the real estate business. It is an adhesive that holds the many parts of your operation together. No matter how small you are, or how large you are, you must advertise through some media, because your advertising program can actually determine the degree of success that you will have toward the objective of your business.

Surveys prove that classified ads reach prospective buyers for a variety of items every day. Therefore, if there's a buyer to be had, the classified columns can reach him.

Put yourself in the shoes of your client. Ask yourself: If you were in the market for a new home, wouldn't you look to the classified columns to see what is available? Let's look at the newspaper from a "reader's view." He buys the paper for one reason, to be informed, not only by the new items, but also by ads. If he is in the market for anything, he knows that the ads will offer him everything "for sale" from a baby carriage to a new home.

*A nationwide eighteen-city survey by the market research reveals:*

1.  Survey showed between seven and eight out of ten buyers mentioned newspapers as their sources for learning about homes or real estate brokers, 18% bought directly from owners.

In Spokane, Washington, a newspaper survey of home buyers showed 90% read the classified ads in their local newspaper—and 87% read them every day while they were house hunting. It took an average of sixteen weeks for a family to find a home.

Real estate brokers themselves report an average of over 80% of their promotional sales dollars invested in local newspapers classified advertising. They have made the local newspapers the natural marketplace for real estate.

There are several unique features of classified advertising that no other media can offer. For example, people seek classified advertising by their own free will. Another feature of classified.

Your ads are consulted by in-the-mood prospects. They read your ads because they want to, at their leisure, when they are in a receptive mood.

That classified advertising lends itself to detailed description in small spaces is another feature. You can illustrate draw word—pictures, describing in detail the outstanding features of a home. Millions of dollars are paid for advertising to secure what the little classified ad gets for such a low cost.

# READERSHIP, ATTENTION, AND SALES RESULTS

There are many ways to make an ad more attractive, more outstanding—to name a few:

1. Use white space wisely...*don't cram the words.*
2. Use a heading that will capture the reader's interest and focus his attention on your ad. There are newspaper companies that provide booklets that contain real estate advertising. These booklets are available at no cost to you.
3. By using large type in your signature, you not only make your ad stand out, but it also institutional in that the readers learn to recognize your ads, and your office.
4. Take advantage of your newspapers company real estate display by inserting house pictures and line drawings of homes floor plans and maps showing directions to display homes.

Probably foremost among the techniques of advertising to secure action and sales results, is the use of "Good Copy." Good Copy can mean the difference between a "quick sale" or "no sale." Good Copy is one of the easiest ways to break down buyers—resistance and to warm up prospects.

Facts, specific information, are important to quick, satisfactory action, and sales results.

# PUT YOURSELF IN THE BUYER'S SHOES

How do we write an ad with good copy? When you are writing your ad, put yourself in the shoes of the buyer, consider the message that you want to tell the reader.

Be as thorough as possible in describing the home. For example, if the home that you have "for sale" has an outstanding feature such as a patio say so, create a word picture.

Give the size, and to add sparkle and effectiveness, you might explain that it is a comfortable place to leisurely entertain guests in the summertime. If the home has a good size yard, say so again, create a word-picture and tell the prospect all the advantages of this particular yard.

Advertisers sometimes complain that they are not getting results from their ads. If I was an owner for a newspaper company, and if an advertiser complains that he is not getting results, I would be interested to find out exactly why he isn't getting results. I would look into the five common reasons for failure of classified advertising to produce results.

1. Is it a product or service for which there is little or no demand? We (would) could hardly blame the classified column for a situation like this.
2. Is the pride of the product or service that is advertised completely out of line? Bear in mind, classified readers are price-keen, and they know if the price is out of line.
3. Did the advertiser make himself available to those who answered his ad? It could be possible that he missed calls if he were not at this phone during the entire day.

4. Did the ad run long enough for the night party to come into the market? Certainly, anyone can understand that the readership of classified advertising on a particular day could not be accurately forecasted. No one can predict what influence the news, the weather, or other factors would have on readership.

5. The most common reason for failure of classified advertising to produce results is "poor copy." As I stated before the copy in the ad can mean the difference between a "quick sale" *or* "no sale" at all.

# YOU MUST CREATE DESIRE

A quick glance at some ads leaves little doubt why they are getting no response. They not only contain poor copy, but every rule in the book is violated.

In a word-picture to a prospect they will describe a lovely home beautifully landscaped, patio, etc., a description that would indeed arouse the curiosity of a prospective home buyer. But why are these features not described to the readers? The common response to this question is the cost. These facts, left out of your ad, could be more costly because they might delay action. Whereas a few extra lines describing these features could result in a quick sale.

In plain words, tell the reader enough so that you create a desire, wet his appetite so that he will call your office and want to see the home. The important points that prospective buyers look for when buying a home are as follows:

1.  The location—most people know just about where they wish to live.
2.  The size of the home—a family that needs a four bedroom home isn't interested in the two or three bedroom variety; therefore, always specify the number of bedrooms in the home.
3.  The price—there are two schools of thought on this subject. There are some realtors who firmly believe that it is better not to include the price or the terms in the ad. Their theory is to have the reader call their office for this particular information, and if the price is not within their price range, they can get their name, and possibly sell them another house that is within their price range.

This theory is often like skating on thin ice, because very often the ad that lacks this information is just skipped over. There are many people who are reluctant to call a real estate office regarding the price of a home. We prefer the second school of thought. We say, put the price in the ad. If a family's financial status only permits a $35,000 home, there is no use having them look at a $55,000 home.

If you do not want to give the selling price, at least give the down payment, or the monthly payments if your state bylaws permits it, but include some information regarding the price so that the reader will know if the home is within reach of the reader.

4. The type of home—here you would want to state if it is a ranch, two-story, split level, etc. If the construction is brick, siding or stucco, or aluminum you might state that the architecture is modern, French, or English in design.

5. The lot size—besides giving the size of the lot, any other information regarding the lot should be mentioned.

6. Convenience—this is a broad term, and can be defined in many ways.

# AVOID FALSE CLAIMS AND EXAGGERATIONS

Regarding the lot and convenience, keep in mind that it's the principles that are important. Extreme and exaggerated claims will make the public skeptical, and will only bring about undesirable results. For example, if the lot is well landscaped say so. However, do not include this if actually the lot has only a few scrawny bushes.

The most popular ad phrase regarding convenience is usually, "within walking distance." Just how many blocks from schools or to the shopping center is considered "within walking distance" would mean a few blocks or less, certainly, it would be walking distance, when in reality, it means a bus or car ride to get there. Thus far, it is pointed out why we should advertise to get the greatest value with our advertising dollar.

We have ascertained that your ad in the classified columns of your daily papers will secure readership, attention, action, and sales results.

# EACH DAY BRINGS NEW PROSPECTS

Last but not least, is the question of when should we advertise: the best time, the best day, as stated previously, the readership of classified advertising for a particular day could not be accurately forecasted.

Testimonials from advertisers prove that there's profit action to be gained every day. There's no particular day that could be called the best, because each day brings new prospects into the market. You are primarily interested in result action. It would be quite costly, if you skipped a day's advertising and missed a prospect for your home.

Regardless of whether you are selling older homes or new homes, whether you are a small or large company, the classified columns of your newspapers can help the success of your business. Your advertising program can determine the degree of success that you will have toward the objectives of your business.

# HEADLINE IDEAS

Ad impact power starts with an effective *headline*. Studies of keyed—copy ads show that the headline often accounts for from 50% to 75% of the effectiveness of the ad. Proof enough that it pays to make the headline on every ad as strongly arresting as possible.

Other research indicates that there are three principle headline appeals:

— self interest .
— curiosity
— news

And they are in that order.

This collection of headlines is to help you by stimulating your thoughts about the vital beginnings of every successful ad.

Some of the heads will just fit properties now listed. Others will suggest specific ideas to adopt for particular properties.

The whole book will save important time, and freshen the outlook of headline writers.

For maximum pulling power:

— Develop a headline to interest the reader
— Built to be lived in
— Dreamy, little cottage with guest house for Granny
— It's young…it's lovely…and it's not engaged
— Good medicine for all the family
— A small kingdom
— He'll be a stay-at-home in this one
— A very plush pad

— Solid as a pyramid
— There's no place like home when it's yours
— Frankly, we are out of adjectives
— You don't have to be rich to buy your way to happier living
— How about an introduction to the very best construction
— You can't beat individuality
— Convenient is the word
— A "Welcome" home
— Designed with the housewife in mind
— Live in the sphere of influence…
— Remember when people smiled? They still do at…
— Isn't this where you'd really like to live…
— For the love of living see…
— Try this for size
— It needn't be so humble
— Be it ever so humble…own your own home
— Mom's house at Dad's price
— Blue Chip home environment
— Kitchen sink included
— A friendly little house
— For the choosey family
— Not fancy, just honey
— Needs elbow grease and your talents
— The world looks brighter from your windows
— Gold and Silver melt away…real estate is here to stay
— The busy man's heaven
— Do you get a headache when you write your rent check?
— Perfect homes in the perfect location
— Give your family the best
— Built for a heap of living
— Children need a big house
— Every room is an invitation
— This house is child-proof
— A home is a savings account
— Country boy at heart? You'll love this
— Live a country club life all year long

— Now your family can live in luxury
— You'll have room to play ball here
— Neighborhood conscious? Where life begins at 55
— Your bank book won't blink an eye
— Children want to enjoy this
— Right neighbors, right value
— Planned for important people
— Your money couldn't buy more happiness
— Should I buy now or wait till prices go up?
— Happy is the home hunter who sees these homes first
— We hate to rave, but…
— Help yourself to leisurely luxurious living
— If where you live is important
— A home of space and comfort
— One visit will convince you
— Unsurpassed elegance…in an unsurpassed location
— Living at its level best
— Wife wanted…with family and charming husband to occupy this
— Wanted…happy renters
— A house that dared to be different
— Your rent dollar will buy this home
— Homes with a future, your future
— Move one more time…to your own home
— The birds and bees enjoy a home…why not you?
— A home is a woman surrounded by a good house
— Pampers your purse
— Open for inspiration
— Modest but cute
— Don't let these homes pass you up
— The address you give with pride
— If you think of your family
— Design to delight…built to endure…priced to please
— The nicest house on the nicest street
— For the woman who has everything, but a home
— To see it is to love it

— Where your children build happy memories
— Home with a priceless look
— Petted and pampered by particular people
— Undeniable lovely…infinitely livable…and this could be for you
— Charm and dollar value you haven't seen in years
— Away from the hub-bub of city living
— Is living near schools important to you?
— Designed to delight the young at heart
— Have you seen this superb new suburb?
— The wife you save may be your own
— How many ways are there to say "perfect"?
— Fourteen karat look
— Woman to woman…don't settle for less
— New paint sparkles on the beauty
— What a wonderful way to live
— This home is more than a home
— Tired of "look-alike" homes?
— Decorator design with family in mind
— A take-it-easy house
— A fine home says a great deal
— Near-new homes with the brand-new look
— This home puts you up where your ambitions are
— Good neighbors for sale
— Like it? Golfers will
— The greatest thrill is rent money invested in your own home
— Your address is important
— Your home is you
— Count your blessings in your own home
— A half-acre of heaven
— One of these should be your home for keeps
— It's good house sense
— Apple pie condition
— See the quiet home in beautiful…
— Bring your bathing suit to…
— Go fishing across the street

— Need paper and paint but…
— Out where it is cool
— Such a wonderful world of difference
— When spacious living matters…
— The door to happiness is the door to your own home
— When you own a spot of land you own a portion of the world
— It's a great world if you live in the right place
— Back yard full of park
— If you like individuality…here it is
— Where happy folks live
— An older home with young ideas
— Now it can be sold
— An invitation to spacious living
— Styled with you in mind
— Talk about clean…this home sparkles
— Stay supporting landlords
— Live better for less in…
— Tree lovers, have you seen…
— Where it's fun for the family to live
— A pure white gem in a setting of pines
— Shattered city nerves?
— Rocking chair kitchen
— A master piece in planning
— A big little house
— Twenty-first century living
— A man's house that women like
— The perfect marriage of land and house
— Live like the Joneses, but for less money
— Most everybody is moving to…
— See this bargain beauty before someone snaps it off the market
— Make the first step to better living… Call us now
— Be first to qualify for (00) year mortgage
— Investigate today
— "Feisty"

— "Fast-foot" it over to (address)
— Don't be sorry next year
— This year it's going for only $00000
— He who hesitates will find sold on his gate
— This may not be on the market long, so better dash on over
— Don't miss this opportunity to own exceptional property easily
— The red carpet is out for your personal inspection tour
— Come in quickly. It's a sound family investment
— Act now. Dial (000-0000)…(name) will pick you up to inspect this home.
— Be the first to qualify for (00) year mortgage
— Investigate today. "Feisty"
— "Fast-foot" it over to (address)

# ARCHITECTURE

- Rambling ranch type home
- A gleaming white stucco bungalow
- You'll live a fresco aplenty in this
- Mediterranean-styled home
- Cool and spacious Bermuda Colonial
- An old home thoughtfully and perfectly restored
- Early New England right here in (town)
- Traditional in spirit and appearance but modem in convenience
- Born yesterday is what we call this fantastically remodeled older home
- Beautifully built around garden-patio area for a Spanish feeling
- Designed with the whole family in mind
- An old home that reflects stability and charm
- A doll house, painted white, trimmed in (color) and set off in an expanse of green lawn
- Romantic, Provincial Normandy
- Compact, modern cottage with the neat, clean lines that only brick can give
- No ups and downs in this compact bungalow
- Sleek-lined contemporary designed for an expanding young family
- Cozy Cape Cod to snuggle around your family
- Proud Colonial with graceful pillars bespeaks your preference for elegance

# BATHROOMS

- There's a splash of color in these bathroom fixtures
- Ceramic tile bath for beauty and ease
- This newly-refinished bathroom looks sparkling new
- Light-flooded mirror to aid your primping
- Eat in finished in smooth, washable, trouble-free wall canvas
- Luxurious sunken tiled shower with frosted glass enclosure
- No bathroom shivers with these built-in electric heaters
- Waterproof wall paper gives design and character to the unique bath
- Splash-proof enclosure for the boy who gives his dog a bath
- Luxurious lavatory with every imaginable built-in (list)

*All the ladies of the house will love the opulent sunken tub and built-in vanity*

- Two handy sinks for the morning march of toothbrush brigade
- No back bending at last…a raised tub for the baby's bath
- Full bath located in hallway to serve (0) bedrooms
- In bright (color)… Color you'll love to live with Gorgeous (color, type) tile bath…quality that last a lifetime
- To make a house a home… Own it
- Stop that leak in your bankroll
- House gourmet?
- Love…at first sight
- A planned community of settled charm, gentle country living

- New beauty outside… New comfort inside
- Dramatic homes for people who want the finest
- It's the cheeriest house, built like Gibraltar
- It ain't fancy but this home is flawless
- Just right…for family comfort
- Move-in-able, a career woman's house
- What are you doing about inflation?
- Easy, carefree way of living
- Does your family deserve a promotion?
- Descriptive Sales Phrases

# ATTENTION GETTERS

- If a man's house is his castle, he should own it
- Growing pains? Stretch out in this spacious home
- A castle for a king and a home for a queen
- An extraordinary house at an ordinary price
- You'll ooh and ahh over this house
- Don't battle—be compatible in this extra-large (0)-bedroom home
- Bring suitcase…this little gem is furnished
- One home value that inflation passed by
- Good homes like this are getting scarcer and scarcer
- Reduce living costs while raising your living standard
- Here's a home that grows with your family
- Pamper yourself. Isn't it time you had a home to be really proud of?
- A hint of nostalgia for our own American yesteryear
- Ole! This home speaks Spanish
- This is one grand buy
- All this and security, too, for only $0,000
- It's a honey for the money
- Why wait to build when you can buy a home like this?
- Own a home…the conqueror of fear

# ACTION URGES

- Be safe today. Don't be sorry tomorrow you missed this terrific home buy
- Value like this sells fast so call this minute
- The early bird will buy this home, so fly out
- See it now—it'll sell fast
- Act now—the red carpet is out
- Pack your bags—you move in today
- Your whole family will live better in…
- Trade up to elegance
- Dutch cleanser bright
- Happiness and good luck for sale
- Jet age efficiency all weather house
- Put your heart and whole family in this happy home
- Homes don't grow but families do
- Young family? Growing children? See this for the wife of an executive
- Don't put off life's greatest thrill
- You've seen the rest… Now see the best
- Building happiness into a home
- The company with prestige…
- Rent donor…or the home owner?
- Do you have "country-itis"?
- For a successful man
- How sweet it is for you and the kids
- It's wife approved
- Enjoy the new sound of a happy family
- Think twice…can you pass up this home?
- Get a whopping income tax refund this year

- A prettier home is mighty hard to find
- We're looking for a special kind of family
- Be sure the house you buy will be a home
- The view goes on and on
- Where everything is new but its trees
- The years and the tenants have been good to this house
- A rare and serene beauty
- Live—where you want to live…
- Don't be chained to an old house
- Paradise for you and your children
- The measure of your success…your home
- Join the happy move to
- Room to room
- Will outlast your grandchildren
- A home with a warm heart
- Love a gracious setting
- Plush as a palace
- Crying on the outside…laughing on the inside
- For the tired or retired
- The house with everything
- Kitchen of beauty and joy forever
- Not just a new home, but a new way of life
- Pride of ownership sparkles in every home
- Where you live makes a difference in how you live
- Custom designed with your type of living in mind
- Heaven on earth for your girl and boy
- Good to the last nail
- The theme here is roominess

# BASEMENT

- Finished basement complete with fireplace for snowy, indoor days
- Smartly decorated entertainment area—in the basement
- Basement complete with convenient, attractive built-in laundry

- Row after row storage shelves
- Ready for work! This basement has a fully equipped handyman's comer
- A basement rumpus room fitted to suit an active host
- Basement remodeled into a jolly recreation room
- Give better and gayer parties in this basement whoopee room
- Finished basement ready for family entertainment area
- Daylight basement with cheery laundry rooms and drying lines
- Convert dry, finished basement into big playroom for the kiddies
- Hideaway storage space a plenty in this huge basement
- Walkout basement is dry, airy, and sunlit
- Bright walkout basement gives you a bonus living area
- Basement designed as a comfortable entertainment area

## BEDROOM

- This is the bedroom you have dreamed about
- A serene master bedroom secluded from living areas
- Your little buckaroos can make a real bunk house out of this corral size bedroom
- A bedroom out of a fairy tale for your little sleeping beauty
- Get away from it all in this cozy, quiet bedroom, the place to retire in luxury
- Waterproof walls in kids' rooms resists Indian attacks!
- High, airy master bedroom evokes a bright mood
- Bedrooms owe their charm to carefully chosen wallpaper
- Paper master bedroom is gay profusion of freshness and flowers
- Designed for privacy…help you escape from the tensions of time
- Surprise bedroom in (color) and (color)
- Traditional (color) wallpaper adds warmth to contemporary bedroom

- Child's bedroom designed for growing and dreaming
- Luxurious master bedroom adjoined by bath and powder room

## BREAKFAST ROOM

- Cozy breakfast nook lends warmth and contentment to meals
- Large breakfast room provides the extra elbow room you need
- Family meals are especially nice in this cheerful nook
- Cheery breakfast room to start the day right!
- A cozy place "Quick"
- A cozy place for "quick bites" and midnight snacks too
- Step saving breakfast bar for mother's busy mornings
- Gay, little breakfast comer for neighborly get-togethers
- Spacious breakfast room double as dining room

## UTILITY ROOM

- No trackin' and sloppin' handy carport leads to utility room
- Gleaming utility room includes built-in storage cabinets!
- Ideal laundry-utility room with planned extra storage
- Utility room holds all laundry equipment
- Well-planned utility room makes wash day almost fun
- Ironing is cool as a breeze in (direction) exposure utility room
- Handy utility room with ample cupboard space

## DEN

- Roomy den with roads of built-in shelves and bookcases
- Privacy for dad in the masculine, paneled den
- Rest to undistracted work or rest in the comfortable air-conditioned den
- Den that's perfect for relaxation, work

- An "at home" study for young scholars
- Sound proof den for the busy executive who needs an office at home
- Spacious den with an extra guest room potential
- Quiet retreat for adults who enjoy good books and good music
- Dad's office away from the office
- This paneled soundproof den affords many hours of enjoyable reading
- Electric outlets just everywhere!
- Wood-paneled den exudes warmth, charm, masculinity
- Just the spot for a friendly poker game
- Convertible den doubles as a charming guest room
- Den that's a haven for dad or homework center for the kids
- Double duty den makes a charming guest room

## DINING ROOM

- A pleasure to accept dinner invitations to this gracious room
- The room that says you're the "hostess with the mostest"
- A perfect room for the art of dinner entertaining
- Dining area opens to outdoor patio...perfect for buffet entertaining
- Meals served in this bright, friendly dining room are extra special
- Guests will enjoy graceful luxury in this formal dining room
- Family meals are special occasions in this early
- American dining room
- Formal dining room has no unsightly view of kitchen
- Traditional dining room to enrich contemporary entertaining
- Formal dining room adds brilliance and sparkle to your most elegant dinners

- You'll be pardonably proud when you invite the girls over… but smile modestly
- Room seasoned for casual family dining or elegant entertaining
- "Behind the wall" shelves provide safe, orderly storage for your fine china
- Enormous old-fashioned dining room perfect for large family get-togethers

## FAMILY ROOM

- A family room of unusual proportion, unusual utility, unusual charm
- A place for your little "rough riders" to romp
- Family room where two generations come alive
- Plenty of hideaway storage for hobbies and games
- A "built-to-take-it" family room for today's casual living
- Convenient family room is playroom by day, party room by night
- Practically decorated family room that's serviceable and suitable to any occasion
- Spacious enough for that informal dance, yet small enough to be cozy
- You and your kids will both entertain in the spacious family room
- Family room lets you segregate TV viewers
- Family room easily converted into sophisticated library-den
- If you're inventive, you'll dream up a great idea for the family room
- Bright extra room perfect for mom's sewing, ironing, and TV
- Your imagination can run wild in this family room
- Husbands and hobbies love this hideaway room
- You and your little finger painters will love this playroom
- Here's hospitality plus for unexpected house guess

# PLUMBING

- Plumbing engineered for easy, low cost installation of automatic washer or dishwasher
- Carefully planned trouble-free septic tank system
- Preplanned plumbing for added low cost bathroom
- Copper pipes throughout for a lifetime of carefree service
- Color coordinated, remodeled bathroom
- Sparkling, durable, and easy-to-clean (Brand) sinks in kitchen and baths
- Lifetime service and satisfaction and (Brand) plumbing fixtures
- Luxury of a sunken Roman tub in decorator (color)

# ELECTRICAL

- Enjoy the flattering softness of indirect lighting
- Enough electrical "house power" for every appliance you can buy
- Convenience and safety of central control panel lighting system
- Get full appliance performance with (000) amp electrical service
- Indirect lighting flatters you…your furnishings
- Designer lighting fixtures for a modern "extra touch"
- Ceiling panel lighting for a bright, workable kitchen
- Electric outlets everywhere…geared to keep pace with your future needs
- Imagine here with the warm glow of the wood-burning fireplace

# FIREPLACE

- Spend happy holidays at your own cherry fireplace
- Surround this warm fireplace with your happy family
- Huge brick fireplace bespeaks a past as America as apple pie

- Real brick...burns real wood
- Copper freestanding fireplace radiates warmth and light
- Dine by firelight with this comer fireplace
- Big brick fireplace is center of family room life

## CARPORT

- Just a touch of your finger and automatic overhead doors open
- Roomy garage with overhead electric-eye door
- Neatly arranged storage in this easy-to-clean garage
- Plenty of room in weather protector carport
- Spacious garage has Dad's workbench already built-in
- Finished garage interior...easy to convert into additional room
- Space for car, storage for tools, sheltered play area for kids in this (size) garage
- Carport entrance keeps you and your car high and dry on rainy days

## FLOORS

- Satin-smooth tinted cement floor in basement, laundry, and clubroom
- Beautifully grained parquet floors reflect your preference for elegance
- Colorful carefree terrazzo for easy living
- The mighty oak...for those magnificent floors
- Luscious, deep-piled (color) carpeting throughout
- Unparalleled (typed) vinyl floor for enduring beauty
- Sculptured elegance with (type) tile
- Seamless kitchen floors stays clean longer
- Durable, mar-proof (type) floors reduce maintenance costs
- Real (type) wood floors...not just floor covering
- These mar and scratch resistant oak floors are easy to keep clean and beautiful

- Mirror-like varnished hardwood floors
- Parquet floors just refinished like factory new
- Character under foot every step in this pegged oak floor
- Elegant (type) floors you'll never want to cover with carpet
- Scuff-resistant, easy-care (type) floors
- Shining oak floors will be your pride
- Work-free terrazzo floors all through the house
- Work-saving modern as tomorrow plastic tile floors

## HALLS

- Spacious hallway provides separate access to each room
- Unusual upstairs hall with plenty of space for extra sleeping
- Smartly designed halls are models of convenience
- Cheery entry hall reflects your friendly "hello"
- Dramatic entry hall with handy storage closet
- Brightly decorated hall gives homey feeling to family and guests
- Useful hallway saves wear and tear on the living room floor
- Cork floors soften footsteps in the softly lighted halls

## CLOSETS

- Lighted closets are handy, convenient
- All closets have convenient folding doors
- More closet space than your husband will let you fill
- Fresh, cedar lined closets give priceless protection
- Clothes are never crushed, wrinkled in king-size walk-in closets
- Moth-tight, hook lined storage closet
- Automatic closet light you can't forget to turn out
- Sliding-mirrored closet doors to delight the fastidious dresser
- Built-in fittings gives closets amazing capacity

## HEATING

- Modern (type) heating takes care of itself
- Clean, modem (type) heating saves you money
- (Type, brand) heating even keeps the basement comfortable
- It's nice to wake up on nippy mornings with (brand) heating
- Cut your fuel bones to the bone with (type) heating
- All season comfort with (type) reverse-cycle system
- Winds of January outside-warmth of June inside
- Individual room thermostat for economy and comfort

## AIR CONDITIONING

- Controlled sleeping comfort every night with (number) air-conditioned bedrooms
- Comfort assuring central air conditioning lets you pick your temperature
- Enjoy cool, clean, dehumidified living in hottest weather
- Centrally air conditioned for maximum comfort and minimum noise
- You can control the climate you live with a flip of the switch
- "Set and forget" year round temperature control
- Healthy, happy summer living in resort cool (brand) air conditioning
- Good by dust, pollen and smoke with centrally-filtered air conditioning

## KITCHEN

- Huge kitchen gives you happy spot for menu planning, telephone and TV viewing
- Where you'll want to plan as well as prepare finer meals
- A kitchen that lightens the labor of company
- A woman's kitchen, with cabinets and electric stove where they should be

- Cook to your heart's delight in this spacious, ultramodern kitchen
- Counter and cupboard space for a banquet
- A girl's best friend is a diamond of a kitchen
- Your "wife insurance" is this easy-to-care for, easy-to-clean kitchen
- Ideal culinary workshop for the gourmet cook
- Cooking peninsula and planned work area big enough for two cooks
- Time saving appliances built into this "wife saving" kitchen
- You'll be a culinary engineer in this supersonic kitchen
- Quick cleaning (type) floors aids busy home maker
- Love to cook but hate to clean up? Handy built-in dish-washer is for you
- Compact as a gallery yet plenty of cupboard space
- Snug eating alcove conveniently close to stove, refrigerator

## LIVING ROOM

- Off-floor, light-scale look of storage wall adds size to living room
- (Size) living room takes beautifully to formal or informal decor
- No hemmed in feeling in this large (size) living room
- Wood see-through grille marks off living room, but pre-serves flow of space
- Large living room divided dramatically by a change of floor levels
- Enjoy the whole garden pool scene from the open living room
- (Type) paneling enhances the charm of this friendly room
- Quiet, tranquil living room with acoustical ceiling
- Space-saving, sliding doors pocket into deep walls
- Majestic beamed cathedral ceiling in living room
- The great outdoors is the great indoors through the com-pliments of large picture windows

- A living room big enough for all your family to really live in
- A living room…ready, willing, and able to live up to his name
- A great place for guests and cozy enough for two
- Chinese Modern and Early American…this room is ready to be custom designed for you

## LOAN ARRANGEMENTS

- Financing this home is easy as financing an automobile
- Just ($000) per month and ($000) down
- Just ($000) down and ($00) per month gives your family the security of their own home
- Some lucky buyer will assume monthly payments of only ($00)
- All it takes to secure this home for your future is ($00) a month
- Trade rent receipts for the deed to do this house. Just ($00) a month
- Only ($000) down payment and assume low interest loan at ($00) a month
- Best of all, it's ($00) a month…cheaper than renting
- Your home ownership dream is real with just $000 down, $00,000 total
- You only pay ($000) down for the pride and comfort of this home
- Here's the perfect remedy for your bargainitis
- No fuss, leave the financing to us
- If you can pay rent, you can own this home. Just ($00) monthly
- It's easy to own this lovely home. Only ($000) down and ($00) per month
- Is money stopping you? Look again…($000) down and ($00) a month!
- It's yours for ($000) down and ($00) a month!
- It's yours for ($000) down and ($00) a month!

# LOCATION

- A vital young family area with lots of neighborhood fun
- Where everyone wants to live…but few have the chance
- Schools for tots through teen conveniently located
- Quiet, secluded (Name) street of fine homes and fine families
- Your children will be surrounded by an ideal neighborhood
- Blocks from convenient (Name) shopping center
- In a secluded neighborhood of successful, well-established families
- A short, pleasant bus ride to downtown
- (#) bus stops just (distance) away
- Where the sun shines brighter and your heart seems lighter
- Just a little this side of paradise
- Where it's mighty good to be when the day is done and shadows fall
- In surroundings you'll long to get home to
- Neat homes and yards reflect community spirit

# LANDSCAPING

- On main highway at excellent spot to attract tourists
- Rolling wooded lot frames this lovely home
- Thoughtful builder saved all the shade tree
- Mature, manicured lawn needs only a minimum of maintenance
- Absolute privacy provided by (type) hedge enclosing whole lot
- Large, tree-covered lot waiting to shelter your home
- The perfect sight for your vacation cottage
- A neat white picket fence sets of the little world that's yours
- The sort of lawn that grows deck chairs and a huge mushroom of an umbrella
- Entire rear yard enclosed by vine-covered trellising
- A yard that's just a little bit of heaven

- A yard where a man can escape from the world
- The giant shade trees are among the neighborhoods oldest inhabitants
- "Pick your own" fruit trees
- A fine garden that a little care can make magnificent
- Fireproof, weatherproof shingles with the mellow beauty of weathered wood
- Fine (00) year (brand) roof has (00) years of guarantee left
- Stone chip surfaced roof reflects heat
- Long lasting beauty with roof of (brand) asphalt shingles
- Wind and weather never bother the lifetime (material) roof
- Your hone's crowning glory...a (type) roof
- Rain or snow, this roof is guaranteed weatherproof for (number) years

## SWIMMING POOL

- The beauty of this (type) roof is only outdone by its durability
- A sun-shrine for the whole family
- Where you'll wish you could linger longer
- (Size) pool in screened patio makes indoor entertaining passe
- With a safety fence for the wee ones
- Enjoy resort luxury in your own home with a (size) pool
- Cure for weekend travel pains...relax in your own pool
- Every day's a holiday with this fun-living (size) pool
- Healthier, happier summers for the whole family with this (size) pool

---

# PART TWO

## HOW TO DO A FEASIBILITY STUDY FOR A PROSPECTIVE INVESTOR

WHAT I HAVE DISCOVERED, ESPECIALLY IN THE
STATE OF MICHIGAN, IS THAT MOST REAL
ESTATE PROFESSIONALS DO NOT KNOW
HOW TO DO A FEASIBILITY STUDY.
THIS SECTION IS SPECIALLY PREPARED
SO THAT THE REAL ESTATE BROKERS AND
THEIR AGENTS CAN IMPROVE ON THEIR
REAL ESTATE SKILLS, AND BETTER SERVE
THEIR CLIENTS, AND IN ESSENCE, ENHANCE
THEIR EARNING POWER. HE OR SHE MUST
FIRST HAVE A CLEAR UNDERSTANDING
OF WHAT A REGION REALLY IS.

# REGIONAL ANALYSIS

Vastly improved transportation and communications at all levels since the end of World War II have brought many changes in life pattern of people and in the geography of their environment. Living customs and business operations now focus around the region where once they centered on the city. Although these changes have exerted a tremendous impact on every segment of the economy they have had a particularly dramatic effect on real estate.

Modern highway systems have been a prime factor in establishing the central city as the hub of an expanding metropolitan area which, in turn, is the focal point of the surrounding region. No longer is it necessary for workers to live in the immediate vicinity of their employment. The commuter rolls are rapidly increasing in direct proportion to improved transportation facilities. Every section of the regional complex is contributing constantly to the social and economic life of the total area.

The continuous ebb and flow of people between cities has created a new growing interdependence between communities. Gone forever is the old concept that a single city within defined corporate geographical limits is sufficient unto itself in providing all of the services, conveniences, and comforts required or desired by local residents. Consider further the fact that a great many businessmen now travel between widespread cities such as Toronto and Vancouver or Montreal and Calgary on an almost weekly basis, to say nothing of more frequent travel between regions two hundred to six hundred miles apart. This growing trend of free movement to obtain new products or labor supply, or to sell to other markets, portends still greater regional expansion, with a corresponding increase in the interdependence of regions.

# WHAT IS A REGION?

Although a region might lend itself to many definitions, it is fundamentally, an area that embraces the maximum practicable number of those elements which, in common, constitute the problem for which the region is being defined. Thus every problem or purpose will delimit its own different area. Geography frequently but not always, will prescribe its limits. Political subdivisions will seldom influence its boundaries. The region is most frequently discussed in relation to commercial areas, and here it is usually referred to as the trading area.

When speaking of markets, the regional area follows closely the pattern of communication and transportation avenues. The region comprising the electric distribution area of the Niagara Falls distribution network is readily understood to transcend many geographical and political boundaries. The commonality of competitive factors are of essential needs are the elements which prescribe the practical limits of a region. (NOTE: At this point the lecturer may wish to discuss briefly the advent of regional government in Ontario, and to try to delineate the particular geographic, political or economic region in which the class works.)

Another example of how a region can be circumscribed by competitive factors of commerce that completely nullify political and geographical boundaries is seen in many suburban regional retail centers. A well-planned and coordinated group of stores in a shopping center located in a satellite area may attract trade from hundreds of small neighborhoods. If this shopping center is contagious to a major metropolitan area, it is noted that its trading area (its market) may extend for twenty to forty miles further into rural areas, but rarely will extend more than three to five miles in the direction of downtown.

The lateral spread of its market region may also be curtailed by a similar adjacent shopping center on the periphery of the metropolitan area as much as five or ten miles away. In describing such a regional area, the real estate man gives far greater weight to commercial limitations of the region than he would to political, geographical, or social boundaries.

Regions, by their nature, are heterogeneous in character, with many pocketed of diverse land use residential, commercial, industrial, recreational, and agricultural. In most cases there is but a feeble relationship between two or more adjoining pockets. This erratic development of the typical metropolitan area, aptly described as urban sprawl, is immediately apparent in the crazy-quilt pattern of a regional land use map.

Local prejudices, varying tax, and assessment practices, and wide differences in local codes and ordinances, combined with a multitude of political differences, are impeding the development of quick and orderly solutions to some of the most vital regional planning problems. But the most serious obstacle is the lack of adequate political machinery to tackle the problems on a regional basis wherever the limits of such regions overlap political boundaries. There are some isolated exception, and it is these that provide a glimmer of hope for what can be accomplished in the future.

For example, Toronto has formed a metropolitan super government over six municipal satellite communities. This, is bringing order into water distribution, sewage disposal, road net, and other common problems. The Northeastern Illinois Metropolitan Area Planning Commission was created by the state legislature to a similar sort of coordination of certain governmental functions for the six counties surrounding Chicago. Such attempts at regional coordination beyond political and geographical boundaries illustrate the all-encompassing point of view necessary in the analysis of factors affecting real estate.

The realtor is no longer necessarily confined to business activities in a given neighborhood or in a single community. He is rapidly becoming a regional broker, not only for additional business opportunities, but because of broaden investment interests and activities of his clients. At the same time, no longer is a neighborhood sufficient unto itself, but dependent on adjoining neighborhoods throughout the region. It becomes obvious that the astute broker is obliged to conduct an intensive regional analysis if he is to understand fully all of the forces that continuously act on a particular investment property in that region.

## Objectives and Uses of Regional Analysis

The regional analysis is an intensive research project from which valuable decisions will be made. For any number of purposes for which the realtor may be called on to make a regional analysis:

1. To determine if a developer should become active in an area.
2. To relate a particular investment property to the entire region.
3. To assist a business or industry in determining future plans for either locating in the area or changing its current method of operations.
4. To assist government in planning public improvements and/or increase public facilities.
5. To analyze the direction of trends which will affect a given property.

These are only a few among a multitude of other valuable purposes. It is therefore of the utmost importance to the usefulness of the final regional report that there be a complete meeting of the minds between the broker-analyst and the client as to the principal objectives of the survey. The objectives of the study must be such that they will justify the time and energy necessary to prepare a comprehensive report.

## Conducting a Regional Survey

In undertaking a regional survey, an essential starting point is preparation of an outline that will indicate the main items requiring study, correlation, and elucidation to justify final conclusions. Many regions—those which are of a complex nature—will require consideration of a substantial number of factors affecting the welfare of that area, while other regions may be adequately analyzed by emphasizing a more limited number of subjects. It depends upon the experience, knowledge, as well as the judgment of the manager-analyst to decide on the most critical influences and to present them in logical and understandable sequence, devoid of "eye-wash," trivia, and verbosity.

The following is a suggested outline for a regional survey. The subjects are not necessarily on the order of their importance or presentation. Neither does the outline purport to be an exhaustive listing of all subjects that might be covered.

# SUGGESTED OUTLINE FOR A REGIONAL SURVEY

1. *Regional Boundaries*

    A. *Stability of the boundaries*
        1. Geographical and topographical
        2. Man-made restrictions

    B. *Explanatory maps and other data*

2. *Regional Land Uses*

    A. Explanatory maps and other data
    B. Restrictive influences area

3. *Economy of the Area*

    A. Principal activities and trends
    B. Competitive influences
    C. Welfare of the economy
    D. Opportunity for growth

4. *Population Characteristics*

    A. Median incomes
    B. Age groups and family sizes
    C. Ethnic groups
    D. Employment
    E. Stability and trends

5. *Communications, Transportation, and Utilities*

    A. Road net maps
    B. Public transportation
    C. Parking
    D. Adequacy of utilities

6. *Real Estate Characteristics*

    A. Types and ages of improvements
    B. Vacancies
    C. Rent ranges
    D. Character of ownerships and real estate activities
    E. New Construction
    F. Public facilities and improvements
    G. Popularity of various neighborhoods

7. *Recreation, Spiritual, and Education Considerations*

    A. Parks and playgrounds
    B. Theatres, athletic events, other entertainment
    C. Hotels and Restaurants
    D. Schools and colleges
    E. Churches

## *On-site Inspection of Region*

The first step in studying a region is a thorough, preplanned personal inspection of the entire area. Advance planning must have the benefit of all available land use maps, zoning regulations, building and housing codes and ordinances, traffic and street maps, and, if possible, contour maps. During the on-site visit, it is important to take careful note of certain characteristics prevalent in each pocket of the region:

A.  *Street and road patterns*
    Classes of buildings
    Physical conditions of the structures
B.  *Activities and characteristics of people using the area*
    Interdependence of neighborhoods with abutting neighborhoods accessibility, public improvements, and recreational facilities

C.  *Available vacant land*
    New construction underway or recently completed

D.  *Growth and development*
E.  *Public acceptance of the neighborhood, and the area* determined by personal discussion with some of the local business proprietors

## Assembling Statistical Data

The second step in analyzing a region is evaluation and correlation of pertinent and statistical data. Population characteristics and trends of the utmost importance, since they are the means by which the effective demand for property use can be realistically determined. Current and foreseeable rent schedules should be considered alongside of building costs and codes and ordinances. Vacancy data is of great concerns to any investor and must be considered in the bright light of immediate past history and current trends. Reliable records on the quantity and quality of the region's use can be secured on the state highway department, utility companies, local chamber of commerce, and municipal and county agencies.

## Regional Characteristics

Third, the regional characteristics must be studied in depth to answer a number of vital questions:

1. Is the region primarily agricultural, educational, recreational, industrial, commercial, residential, governmental, or devoted to service activities?

2. In which direction or directions is the region growing?

3. What are the regional boundaries, and are they limited by natural barriers, such as high mountains and bodies of water, by immovable man-made barriers (forest preserves, recreational areas, green belts, etc.), or by other restricting influences?

## Economic Considerations

Finally, serious thought and study must be given to the overall economics of the area. A fair and supportable estimate must be made of both the current and foreseeable economy of the region, together with an analysis of relationship between the region's economy and its population. This will involve not only a study of the region itself, but also some realistic research on competition from other regions. Good examples are the competition of the West Coast region's with Atlantic Coast regions in ship-building and the regional competition throughout the nation for industries such as electronics and aircraft and allied products.

The permanency of any large-scale operation is extremely important to the economy of that region. For instance, it is well-known what happens to the Seattle region when its major aircraft industry loses or wins a substantial contract. It is obvious that a well-integrated region enjoying a wide diversity of activity is blessed with the highest degree of economic stability and therefore becomes more attractive to the real estate investor. Under ordinary circumstances, regional areas like Montreal and Toronto are possessed of sufficient diverse activities so that a lull in any single activity does not vitally affect the regional economy. On the other hand, cities like Oshawa and Windsor are economically dependent to a very large extent on one or two primary activities.

The time and effort invested in the regional study must assure the best possible estimates of all contributing factors, with their relationship to the analyst's conclusions and recommendations clearly defined in the final report.

# FORMAT OF THE WRITTEN REPORT

The organization of the completed report should be such that the client can quickly and easily refer to the subjects that interest him. The sequence should be such that the reader will be led into the analyst's final conclusions.

Here is the suggested sequence of a typical report:

1. Title page
2. Letter of transmittal briefing the objective and major final conclusions
3. An aerial photograph of the region
4. Table of contents
5. Narrative of the purpose of the report
6. Detailed description of the region as to its boundaries
7. Statement of restricting influences
8. Regional land uses
9. Real estate characteristics
10. Population characteristics

11. Communications, transportation, and utilities
12. Area economy
13. Recreational, spiritual, and educational considerations
14. Correlation of all influences to the objective of the report
15. Conclusions and recommendation order of importance
16. Qualifications of the analyst

*Statements of fact and statistical data must be supported by source references.*

Where a statement is the analyst's opinion, it should be so identified and an explanation given for its basis. The regional analysis is far too important a document for off-the-cuff judgments or opinions that are no more personal impressions that can't be substantiated. Conclusions and recommendations must be totally devoid of personal prejudices and wishful thinking, but they should embrace the attitude of conservative optimism rather than reluctant pessimism.

A regional survey is necessarily a major undertaking. Under ordinary circumstances it can be completed in about five intensive working days, provided that the analyst is working in a region with which he is completely familiar. For an unfamiliar area, about eight working days are involved. When the objectives require an unusual broad study, including a vast amount of personal contact, polling of opinions, and outside professional assistance, the time factor can run into a month or longer.

When the broker undertakes a regional analysis, he must keep in mind that he is withdrawing himself temporarily from most other gainful efforts. In establishing his fee for the preparation of an analysis, consideration must be given to the amount of time consumed and the expenses incurred. There should be no reticence in charging a fair fee; the serious client will never question a proper charge if he is fully informed on the involvement of the analyst.

The majority of clients who contract for regional analyses want to know in advance what their financial commitment will be. They rightfully anticipate that the realtor has a sufficient amount of experience to furnish this information. It is always difficult to suggest how the exact fee for a regional analysis should be established where the contributing factors are so variable. A first-class job will always justify attractive reward, and broad experience becomes increasingly valuable.

Example: *Feasibilities*
1. Objectives
2. Market trend
3. Legal political constraints
4. Esthetic ethical constraints
5. Physical technical constraints
6. Financial constraints

# COMMERCIAL REAL ESTATE

This session flows naturally from the previous sessions which were concerned with regions. The session concerns itself with the study of the feasibility of a project.

## Feasibility Studies

One of the most valuable and rewarding efforts in which the realtor is singularly and eminently qualified is the conduct of feasibility studies for proposed investment properties.

Fundamentally, the studies are economic in nature, measured in term of supportable estimates of net cash flow as related to total construction costs; land value; highest and most productive land use; and directly related to the present and foreseeable real estate market. This is no easy task even for the experienced practitioner and it is next to impossible for the layman or neophyte.

The preparation of a useful feasibility study involves searching analyses of reliable information and data in many directions. It must be completely devoid of emotionalism, unsupportable guesses or assumptions, and impulsiveness. It must be approached with cold logic and recorded in good sequence. It must be easy to read and understand. It must be brief as possible yet it must not avoid essential detail.

The feasibility of an investment project depends not only upon a wide spectrum of economic (and sometimes social and political) factor but it also relies upon a realistic forecast of future potential. Pertinent data must be gathered from authentic statistics accurately interpreted; dependable performance records for comparable properties; intensive market research, and a broad experience in the market place. Depth of demand, current and foreseeable competition, and user capabilities are salient considerations in evaluating the gross income stream. The long list of operating expenses must be carefully stabilized and tabulated. Financing must be explored in the market place to determine the availability of suggested borrowings. Finally, the net cash flow must be analyzed to conclude whether or not the net yield indicates justification for implementing the project.

It has become regrettably obvious that a great many projects have been completed without benefit of an authoritative feasibility study which would have wisely discouraged almost certain failures. As a result there is a spiraling demand for such studies for the benefit of developers, investors and mortgage lenders. With the above thoughts in mind it becomes important that a comprehensive set of processes and procedures be adopted for the preparation of a feasibility study. The study begins with the regional analysis discussed in the last session.

# NEIGHBORHOOD ANALYSTS

Every property belongs to a neighborhood and that neighborhood creates the environment which determines the probability of success in a proposed project. Unless the neighborhood is transitional in character, great care must be exercised to make certain the proposed development is neither an over-improvement nor an under-improvement for the neighborhood.

To establish a clear concept of the neighborhood it is essential to identify its boundaries and the kind of uses properties are put to in the neighborhood. Once again, caution is suggested in looking for any transitional trends which might suggest changes of use in the foreseeable future.

The neighborhood is probably our most familiar geographic entity. We all grew up in neighborhoods, we visited other neighborhoods and we subconsciously identified the characteristics of neighborhoods.

Our studies must include the population characteristics such as age groups, ethnic groups, family incomes, employment statistics, and other salutary activities of people if we are concerned with residential development primarily.

# COMMERCIAL REAL ESTATE SESSION No. 3
## *THE SHOPPING CENTER*

### PART 1

## DEVELOPING THE SHOPPING CENTER

Shopping centers are not new in concept. The first shopping centers were the marketplaces where people gathered regularly for the sale and exchange of merchandise, and around which towns and cities grew up. Archaeologists have discovered the ruins of a shopping center that existed. More than 1,700 years ago in Sardis, the capital of Lydia, where the fabled King Croesus reigned. We can easily see our present downtown areas as overgrown shopping centers. And modem-day living, characterized by the trend toward decentralization, has given rise to a new type of shopping center.

Many people experienced in general real estate believe that shopping center development and management may be compared to other types of real estate investment. There are, however, several important points of difference that deserve study. This session will consider these unique characteristics as they relate to planning of a successful shopping center investment project.

# INTRODUCTION

**SCOPE**: The realtor who attempts to make a presentation on a proposed shopping center consisting only of a map, a photograph, and a traffic count is as outdated as the horse and buggy. Today's development, management, and sale of shopping centers is a highly specialized business. During the preconstruction stages of a large shopping center, the following technical experts are customarily retained:

| | |
|---|---|
| Market Analyst | Traffic Engineer |
| Site Planner | Real Estate Broker |
| Merchandising Consultant | Project Architect |
| Landscape Architect | Mechanical Engineer |
| Electrical Engineer | Legal Counsel |

*Canadian Outlook*: The development of major shopping centers in Canada has become so specialized that a limited number of consultants account for substantially all of the site location, site development, merchandise planning, and shopping center lease negotiations. This does not exclude the local realtor, but rather tends to provide him with a knowledgeable and cooperative ally in exploring potential shopping center sites. Owners, developers, and lending institutions prefer to deal with these consultants for several reasons:

1. *Experience*—their training precludes the making of most obvious development errors and many detailed and obscure ones.
2. *Lease Negotiations*—they have an entree to all merchandising chains and a negotiating background that obtains maximum rental rates and favorable terms.
3. *Impartiality*—they are not identified locally with any one site, community, or group of officials.

4. *Financing*—they know the institutional lenders, other sources of funds and in addition to knowledge of methods of meeting shopping center financing requirements.

5. *Technical knowledge*—usually have engineering, architectural, and/or legal background with practical application to shopping center problems.

These specialists are often Canadian firms retained on a fee basis and they cooperate willingly with local realtors requiring assistance or advice.

*Terminology*—the following definitions are those provided by the Urban Land Institute:

*Shopping Center*—is a group of commercial establishments planned, developed, owned, and managed as a unit with off-street parking provided on the property and related in location, size, and type of shops to the trade area that the unit serves generally in an outlying or suburban area.

*Site Area*—the gross land area of the property measured in either square feet or structures.

*Building*—Are the ground area covered by the enclosed structure or structures.

*Gross Floor*—Area total floor space of all buildings in a shopping center project including basements and upper floors, but excluding malls for common use.

*Rental Area*—the part of the gross floor area used exclusively by the individual tenants.

*Sales Area*—rentable area minus storage space.

*Parking*—Are the area taken up for car parking including railways, aisles, stalls, islands, and other features incidental to parking.

*Parking Ratio*—the relationship between space required for the parking area and the gross floor area of the buildings, sometimes related to gross usable area minus dead storage area.

# DESCRIPTION OF CENTER TYPES

There is no consistent description or definition of centers. Some texts refer to centers by size, others by types of stores and still others by floor space. The following functional classifications include estimates of size, type of store, etc. The categories described are for general definition only. In practice, each center is different and must be tailored to the specific prevailing circumstances. Its final form is only ascertained after detailed surveying and analysis. However, the three general classifications listed below are natural groupings and are useful distinctions:

1. **Neighborhood Center**
   a. convenience goods center
   b. 30–75,000 square foot gross floor area.
   c. major tenant food market
   d. minimum site area: 4 acres
   e. minimum support: 1,000 families, 7,000–20,000 people.
   f. sells primarily groceries, hardware, drugs, some service, beauty parlors, cleaners, etc.
   g. 10–15 stores
   h. driving time: 6 minutes.

2. **Community Center**
   a. shoppers goods center
   b. 100,000–300,000 square foot ground floor space.
   c. major tenant variety store or junior department store

  d. minimum site area: 10 acres

  e. minimum support: 5,000 families: 20,000–100,000 people

  f. sells also soft lines (wearing apparel) and hard lines (hardware, appliances)

  g. 20–40 stores

**3. Regional Centers**

  a. shoppers goods center

  b. 400,000 square foot of ground floor space.

  c. major tenant one or two department stores.

  d. minimum site area: 40 acres.

  e. minimum support: 70,000–100,000 families, 300,000 or more people.

  f. goods in great depth and variety

  g. 50–100 stores

  h. pulling power based on capacity for comparative shopping modified by time spent in travel with least irritation.

  i. comes closest to reproducing facilities once available only in downtown areas.

# PARKING FACILITIES

Shopping center customers reach the center principally via private automobile transportation. Therefore, centers are customarily located along vehicular road nets leading to and from concentrations of residential population within certain feasible geographical limits, depending on the type of center. Private transportation means parking, and one of the most attractive features of the modem shopping center is convenient and adequate parking.

Initially, a limited number of parking spaces were considered adequate to meet the needs of the center. But as the decentralization trend accelerated and as the popularity of shopping centers grew, more and more parking space became essential not only for customers, but also the rising army of employees. The first step was to establish a ratio between parking and selling space. "One for one" (one square foot of parking for each square foot of selling space) became an early standard. It was not too long before the formula became "two for one" (two square feet of parking for each square foot of selling space), and finally "four to one" became necessary for full exploitation of the larger centers.

As the need grew for more parking space, the total land area required for a center mushroomed to a point where more serious and scientific planning was essential. Studies were made to determine parking habits, the distances people will walk, and the number of spaces needed for various types of business. One result was location of employee parking on the peripheral boundaries of the center. It was found that service stores such as clearing establishments, beauty shops, post offices, banks, real estate offices, and repair shops do not depend on concentrated shopping traffic.

Their customers visit the stores for relatively short times and therefore require only a limited number of spaces. On the other hand, it was found that department stores, variety stores, hardware and house-ware stores, specialty shops, markets, and eating establishments require heavy shopping traffic and attract customers for relatively long periods of time. Thus, these enterprises require substantial parking facilities reasonably close at hand. In all instances, ingress and egress must be convenient, and the parking location must be easily identified. As many spaces as possible should be located as close to the merchants' front doors as practical.

## SITE STUDY

The ideal shopping center site will have certain desirable characteristics. Most sites are not ideal, but have a number of these qualities and some compensation for those that are lacking.

The following points are locational considerations in site selection.

1.   Access—there must be free flow of traffic throughout the feeder area.
2.   Shape—must be shaped so that the ultimate development is all in one piece, undivided by highways or important through traffic streets (this principle is often violated).
3.   Area—sufficient for initial development with room for expansion and buffer strips.
4.   Topography—level or gently sloping is best. Steep slopes, low lying or swamps add to complications in construction.
5.   Utilities—close proximity to water, sewer, gas, and electricity, etc., cuts down on off-site improvements.
6.   Favorable Zoning—climate for good public relations.
7.   Adjacent Land Usage—a meadow may be pretty to behold, but it does not generate walk-in trade.
8.   Price—a variable.

While these principles apply to all centers, the importance of each will be indicated by the particular requirements being studied.

# SITE AND RELATED REQUIREMENTS

To become an attractive investment, a shopping center must possess all of the essentials for economic soundness and stability. Therefore, a natural step in planning such a project is an exhaustive study to determine with reasonable certainty that land conforms to the overall requirements of the completed center. The use of the land for anticipated purposed must conform to existing or attainable zoning and code requirements. The contour of the land for anticipated purposes must be such that the site preparation is feasible and economic. Size of the total site must be adequate for the planned development, with consideration to reasonable adequacy for expansion.

The shape of the site must allow for construction for the facilities in such a manner as will yield maximum utility and economic benefits. Since every shopping center is dependent upon vehicular traffic, its site must be located in accord with existing or definitely programmed road and highway nets leading to and from population areas where potential customers are located. In other words, the shopping center must satisfy a need compatible with trading area in which it is located.

There are certain restrictive qualities for the site of it is to become attractive and useful. Since customer convenience is the key to shopping center success, the site must be in the parcel and not broken up by railroad rights-of-way, public roads, ravines, or other obstacles that will interfere with the free movement of shoppers. In order to intercept moving traffic, the site must enjoy "out look" that is, it should not be located in a hollow where it can be seen only close at hand, but rather it should present an attractive picture from long distances, where the entire project can be readily observed and identified.

Even the most desirable parcel of land that meets all of these requirements can become difficult for development and unattractive as an investment if all factors are not carefully considered in advance of acquisition and construction,

For example, good drainage is vitally important to the entire center, and the ready availability of sewer facilities an all necessary utilities is imperative. The cost of securing these must be carefully considered in preliminary analyses. Time is expensive and must be carefully planned to make certain that no extraordinary time lags will occur to delay completion. Detailed advance planning and a realistic predetermined timetable are essential. Site acquisitions, land clearance and site preparation, installation of utilities, completion of plans, promulgation of the leasing program, and actual construction all are time consuming an require constant study and attention to assure that their schedules are coordinated.

All too often some aspect of the program can delay completion to the point where the economics of the project are seriously impaired.

# PART TWO

If we are considering an industrial project our thinking is directed to other industrial activity, opportunity for expansion, available labor supply and housing for employees, transportation facilities, utilities and utility costs, and all other factors for or against industrial development including the general character of abutting neighborhoods. If our assignment is to study the feasibility of a commercial project, we are concerned with traffic, transit, parking, attractiveness and public acceptance, and competitive aspects.

Regardless of the types of uses superimposed upon our analyses, we are alert to the physical aspects of the neighborhood since these exert a strong influence upon the probability of project success. New improvements and opportunities for new improvements are important indicators of trends. The age of buildings and renovation completed, or in progress, are meaningful plus factors. Public improvements, facilities, and amenities are of material concern and must be critically analyzed.

We then turn to the crucial matter of neighborhood economics and we record and support conclusions in such matters as rentals and demand factors, vacancies, real estate activity, mortgage loan availability, zoning and building codes, construction costs, trends, and public acceptance.

HERMAN R. WILLIAMS

# ANALYSES FOR THE PROPOSED PROJECT PLAN

Now that we have become clearly conscious of the fabric with which we are working, we are prepared to get down to cases and analyze the proposed project. This analysis must be complete in every respect if we are to enjoy a logical conclusion which will, in all probability, lead to a very substantial commitment of money. It is here that we combine our preliminary studies of the region and the neighborhood as related to the proposed project.

## THE SITE

Obviously, our first consideration is the site about which we ask ourselves certain vital questions:

1.  Is its size and shape adequate, too small or too large for the proposed project.
2.  Does the topography present any serious site preparation difficulties?
3.  Has soil condition engineering disclosed any particular construction problems, which will add materially to construction costs?
4.  Is the land zoned for the proposed use?
5.  Is the value attributed to the land for market value?

## ECONOMIC ANALYSIS

In order to work from a firm base we must now proceed to a market analysis directly related to the project. Initially we must determine the inventory of competitive units, their respective rent ranges; the services and facilities included in the rents or charged

70

extra; the age and condition; and the vacancy percentages. The selection of truly competitive units is of prime importance.

Next is an intensive study as to depth of demand. This dictates a jaundices eye scrutiny as to the compatibility of the proposed project with the general characteristics of the neighborhood; a very realistic analysis of the permanent of use for the proposed project units; and comprehensive determination of the capabilities of potential users.

Finally, a look at the future will foretell the probabilities for success or failure. A sound and supportable assessment of trends must direct this approach and serious attention is required as to possible future competitive factors. To adequately forecast what might occur, a complete "look around" is suggested to determine:

a.    What other sites are available for a competitive project?

b.    Would a similar project or series of projects built elsewhere in another neighborhood effectively compete, and are sites available in what might be termed "competitive" neighborhoods? A third question might also be asked: Would additional competitive projects help or hinder the economic success of the proposed project? Although it is agreed that an economic analysis is at best, an informed guess, professional training and broad experience should provide sufficient background for heavily weighted chances in arriving at sound conclusions.

## OPERATIONAL ANALYSIS

Undoubtedly the cash flow projection for the completed project is one of the master keys that will disclose whether or not the project, as conceived, is economically feasible. This is probably the single area in which the professionally competent analyst can fully utilize his records and experience with a high degree of authoritative accuracy. In spite of the fact that the arithmetic might be provable in the real estate market and among other executive managers, it is suggested that the written report contain as much supporting data as possible. This might be accomplished by reference to other sections of the report which contain adequate explanations. The process of preparing this part of the study is mainly one of tabulation (in detail), addition and subtraction, but it must be done accurately, in logical sequence, and it must be all-inclusive.

First a detailed analysis of probable income is set down. This should be prepared on a unit-by-unit basis setting forth unit sizes, special features, if any, and concluded rentals for each unit. From the total projected rents a realistic vacancy (rent loss) percentage should be deducted resulting in a subtotal of projected gross effective rental income. To this subtotal is added informed estimates of other income for items not included in the projected rentals, such as utilities, parking, vending machines, etc. The final total will be the stabilized gross effective rent projected.

The next consideration is operating expenses. This schedule must include every item of expense attributable to normal building operation. A grouping of expense types is recommended. Although all types of projects might not include every suggested expense item, a checklist is very useful to insure that no item is overlooked.

A sample checklist is as follows:

1. **Taxes**
    a. real estate
    b. personal property

2. **Insurance**
    a. fire and ice (amount of annual premium cost)
    b. public liability and a property damage
    c. (amount and annual premium cost)
    d. workmen's compensation
    e. rental (amount and annual premium cost)
    f. employees' bonds
    g. theft, pilferage, and larceny
    h. boiler and mechanical equipment
    i. plate glass
    j. miscellaneous

3. **Wages and salaries**

    Identification of each class of employee; annual gross salary; other compensatory; payroll taxes and charges paid by employer; and other fringe benefits—Christmas bonuses, vacations, and sick leave.

4. Utilities
    a. electricity and power
    b. fuel
    c. water
    d. telephone (on premises)

5. **Contract services**
    a. elevator maintenance
    b. gardening and landscaping
    c. pest control
    d. grounds maintenance
    e. rubbish removal
    f. snow removal
    g. equipment inspection, repair and maintenance
    h. security
    i. miscellaneous

6. **Repairs and replacements**
    a. electrical
    b. plumbing and heating
    c. ventilation and air conditioning
    d. furniture and furnishings
    e. general

7. **Painting and decorating**
    a. interior
    b. exterior

8. **Supplies and equipment**
    a. janitorial

    b.   maintenance and repair
    c.   miscellaneous

### 9. Miscellaneous
    a.   licenses and permits
    b.   incidentals

### 10. Administrative
    a.   management (executive)
    b.   legal
    c.   auditing
    d.   membership and subscriptions
    e.   advertising and public relations
    f.   miscellaneous

When this list has been completed, it should be totaled and subtracted from gross effective income projected to establish net cash flow before mortgage loan service depreciation or income taxes.

If the property is to be encumbered with a mortgage loan, the annual total of required principal and interest payments should be deducted from the net cash flow calculated above, to slow the net cash flow, before depreciation and income taxes, on the equity investment.

## FEASIBILITY OF PROPOSED PROJECT

Attention is now directed to the process of analyzing economic feasibility. Cash flows have been adequately calculated and projected and we have arrived at the point of decision. However, further critical calculations are necessary to arrive at the final cost. Unless the project is 100% leased at the outset, a realistic estimate must be made as to the out of pocket costs until a break even has been reached between income and cash outlay. With this in mind, no real cost items can be overlooked or estimated by frivolous nationalization. The cost component list is on and for simplicity's sake the following items must be adequately enumerated:

1.  Site cost. This can be either the actual cost of acquisition or the value required by the developer.
2.  Site preparation.
3.  Contract cost for the improvements including itemized costs for such chattels to be included as draperies, carpets, television antennae, etc.
4.  Architectural and engineering services including but not limited to soil tests, structural design, heating, ventilation, air conditioning, electrical, etc.
5.  Real estate consulting, feasibility studies, and other professional services.
6.  Title costs, completion bonds, permits, recording costs, etc.
7.  Financing costs interim and take out.
8.  Landscaping.
9.  Janitorial and maintenance equipment and supplies.
10. Legal and accounting services.
11. Leasing, advertising and promotion.
12. Carrying costs to break even which includes a reliable estimate of necessary cash in excess of any collected rentals after paying all calculated operating costs and finance charges.

The sum of these twelve items determines the final total project cost. With this cost as a denominator and the net effective rent before depreciation and income taxes, the percentage return is arrived at. It is this percentage return that determines feasibility when compared with the current real estate for comparable properties. It also dictates the final conclusions and recommendations. The feasibility study objective has been reached!

In the interest of completeness it is suggested that at the end of the report calculations be made to fix the breakeven point before and after income taxes with an estimate of time starting from date of completion until this point is reached.

It is very helpful to include an appendix in the report including such things as: a site plan; a neighborhood plan; schematic drawings of the proposed improvements and other supporting reference data.

A complete feasibility study based on the facts of economic life is the key to successful development and it is a profitable effort for the qualified real estate person who has the tools and knows how to use them.

# COMMERCIAL REAL ESTATE
## SESSION No. ONE
## THE OFFICE BUILDING

### THE DEVELOPER'S VIEWPOINT

The rising demand for business space in concentrated areas combined with technical advances in construction methods and materials have fathered the modem office building as we know it today. From the beginning, office buildings have continually sought to enhance the attributes of location, amenities, and facilities with a maximum of available operation space without prejudice to adequate public areas and internal transportation. Thus, safety, light, ventilation, utilities, facilities and services are all combined in the modem office building to attract desirable tenants at attainable rentals.

The success of a new office building begins at the earliest planning stage and continues through until the doors open to the first tenants. The experienced realtor's active participation in this process form beginning to end is essential if the highest and most productive uses of the project are to be obtained; the owner-architect-broker team is essential to a successful enterprise.

Although numerous variables must be considered in planning a new office building, there can be little doubt that location, architectural design, and economic feasibility are the controlling factors.

This chapter will examine each of them from the standpoint of insuring the maximum value and economic life of the project.

## LOCATION

Location must conform to the demands of the types of business and professional enterprises that can reasonably be expected to utilize what the new building will offer in the way of space, services, amenities, and facilities. In addition, the neighborhood must be compatible and convenient to prospective users. While many different areas of a community can offer suitable locations for office building development, primarily the centers and subcenters of population concentration are most desirable.

Since this discussion is considering the office building designed for general rather than specific purpose, the location close to or within the central core must have first priority, for it is here that the strongest demand for space exists. General office both compliments and supplements retail and other business activities where close proximity is almost a necessity.

## FACTORS IN SELECTION

The selection of a location for a business office varies with the needs of the particular business office operation. These factors are most frequently considered when seeking a suitable location for a business office:

1. proximity to other company operations
2. proximity to services banks, legal, consulting, etc.
3. proximity to customers or supplies
4. proximity to related businesses
5. proximity to labor supply
6. proximity to transportation, shopping, recreation, clubs, etc.
7. prestige
8. cost of occupancy
9. parking

It is significant that six of the above factors are based on "proximity to" or "nearness." In five of the factors proximity to other people is the prime consideration.

Business is people. People in business must communicate with each other. The most effective communication between people is face to face contact. So need for face to face contact has a strong influence in the selection of the location for a business operation. As a result many office operations are established in or near a building which houses the main activity of the organization, e.g., a manufacturing plant, a university, a hospital, a legislative building, a department store. This "efficiency of nearness" is a major factor in selecting the location of a business office operation; provided that accommodation available is otherwise suitable, it is probably the most important factor.

Most businesses locate their head office operation in the central area of a major city where they have the advantage of close proximity to financial, legal, consulting, and other business services with which the corporate executives require frequent contact.

Some businesses, such as life insurance companies establish many branch sales offices in close proximity to their customers. Their head offices are frequently located in the community where the business was established.

Because the factors which are important in selecting a location are common, most business offices tend to congregate in those areas which proximity to these contacts are necessary to business office operations. As a result office buildings tend to develop in closely-knit communities are often "financial district" or the "general insurance community."

As a consequence of these "location" factors, the office building industry tends to be a "big city" activity. Office buildings in the big city area accommodate business activities which are the center for a much broader area than the municipality in which they are located. The extent of this broader area serves as the head office or base of operations. Many insurance companies, banks, manufacturing organizations with head office operations in Toronto and Montreal have a nationwide, or intercontinental, operation.

# INCREASED NEED

The increase of office space per capita in a major city may be illustrated by the growth of the office building industry in the Metropolitan Toronto area.

For the purpose of this analysis, the population base for the broader area for which Toronto is the commercial center is assumed to be the Metropolitan Census Area which extends from Oakville to Ajax and north to Richmond Hill. For this area we have estimated office space per capita as follows:

| Year | Population | Total space (estimate sq. ft.) | Office space (space per capita) |
|------|------------|--------------------------------|---------------------------------|
| 1951 | 1, 210,000 | 9,600,000 | 8.0 sq. ft. |
| 1966 | 2,150,000(est.) | 24,000,000 | 11.0 sq. ft. |
| 1971 | 2,500,000(est.) | 31,000,000 | 12.5 sq. ft. |

During the five-year census period, 1956–1961, the population of the city of Toronto increased by less than 5,000 people. However, in this same period the population of the Metropolitan Toronto Census Area increased by 325,000 people and office space in the City of Toronto increased by over 5,000,000 square feet.

In our present economy total demand for office space is basically a function of

a) Population growth
b) Business expansion
c) The increase in proportion of people employed in office work
d) The extension of the commercial influence ratio of office space per capita

Present demand reflects growth expansion in all four factors. To meet this demand more and more office buildings will be built most of it in the larger cities and in the downtown districts of these cities.

The cycle for the planning, development, construction and leasing of an office building may be a period of two to five years or longer. The Empire State Building in New York opened May 18, 1931. Although construction was completed in a year, and assembly and planning activities were carried out for some years prior to that date, it was 1941 before management completed the leasing of the 1,790,433 square feet of rentable office space.

This serves to illustrate the long term cycle characteristic of the office building industry. The larger the building, the longer the period of planning, development, construction, leasing, and showing a profit in the investment.

Since the demand for office space is closely related to the level of economic activity a "boom" period encourages developers and institutions to launch new office building projects. When an economic downturn occurs many of these projects have difficulty in finding tenants for the new office space they have created.

A study of the office space market reveals recurring periods of oversupply. These tend to discourage new office building projects which are deferred until demand creates a more favorable market. However, because the office building industry has such a long term cycle it sometimes occurs that a lessee's (or lessor's) market will continue for two or three years before a healthy market balance is restored.

# ECONOMIC FEASIBILITY

The economics of planning are concerned with maximum attainable rental income as related to minimum expense without prejudice to top flight maintenance and operation and with full consideration of the market and all competitive factors. Economic feasibility should be the determining factor in all decisions made in project planning.

*Surveying the space and rental market:*

In examining the market for office space, primary consideration should be given to:

1.  The rate and quantity of demand by new businesses in the area.
2.  The rate and quantity of expansion of existing area tenancies.
3.  The quality and quantity of existing area tenants who desire to move to newer, more efficient, more attractive, and more convenient quarters.

Tenancies procurable from the area must be studied carefully, since there is a continuing attrition of occupied office space from tenant movement through going out of business in the area, through movements to institutional buildings, through reductions in office space requirements, or simply through the urge to move. These findings naturally will indicate the extent to which new buildings might be expected to "feed" on the older, obsolescent structures. This underscores further the importance of intensive market studies.

The number of square feet of space for which occupancy may be contemplated must be estimated as accurately as possible. Realistic rentals for that space must be determined based on the going rate for space in the more modern buildings with equal facilities and comparably located in the area.

The unit sizes to be planned must be based on the depth of capable demand. A policy of leasing only on a full floor basis would severely limit the list of prospective tenants, in most cities there is not a sufficient number of large tenants to support such planning. Long experience has proved that the most practical approach is to construct each floor area on a module basis, wherein the placement of utility outlets permits partitioning and subpartitioning almost at will to accommodate the requirements of almost any tenant, regardless of the total space requirements.

Prior to any final determination of rentals, policy must be established as to the amount of improvement and furnishing that will be supplied to individual tenants, such as utility costs, window cleaning, and special service.

## ESTIMATING RENTAL LOSS RATIO

No building enjoys 100% continuous occupancy over any period of years. Thus, once a rent schedule has been established, it must be properly discounted by an allowance for rent loss due to vacancy, tenant turnover, etc., based on experience of comparable buildings. For example: out of a total of 2,000,000 square feet (10%) may be vacant. On the other hand, out of 1,000,000 square feet in the new buildings, there may be only 5,000 square feet (5 %) vacant. Yet, overall vacancy for both types of buildings viewed together will appear as 205,000 square feet, or (7%) of the 3,000,000 square feet total.

To arrive at a true measure of rent losses, the planner must add to the vacancy rate a fair allowance for tenant turnover, bad credit, legal costs, lease commissions, and untimely decorating expenses.

HERMAN R. WILLIAMS

# THE ECONOMICS OF A
# HYPOTHETICAL BUILDING

To illustrate the process of determining the economic feasibility of an office building, let us make a few basic assumptions that will permit us to prepare a hypothetical analysis.

Study has led to the conclusion that a site available in the center of the central city financial district is most suitable for a moderate size office structure. Since office sizes and layout cannot be determined in advance, construction should be on a four-and-one-half foot module open floor basis. (Each module, or unit area, will contain available utilities.) Maximum rentable space with the greatest possible operating efficiency will result from a central-core type structure, in which elevators, stairwells, public areas, and janitorial facilities will be at the center surrounded by rentable office space. Climate conditions and competition require heating and air conditioning facilities.

It is foreseeable that 300,000 square feet of upper floor office space can be absorbed within a reasonably short period. Construction costs, including all carrying charges, architects fees, etc., will be approximately_____ per square foot of total building area, allowing for necessary basement storage space. Garage parking facilities are required for a minimum of 300 vehicles at a cost of $15.00 per square foot for 90,000 square feet. Careful market studies indicate an average rental of $7.00 per square foot per year for office space and $360.00 per year per garage space.

The total lot area is 22,500 square feet, 150 feet fronting on the street by a uniform depth of 150 feet. Zoning laws permit land coverage of 20,000 square feet overall. The best architectural planning will allow for 7,000 square feet of ground floor store space at a market rental of $12.00 per square foot per year. Gross area for the entire structure, including ground floor stores, in 400.000 square feet, plus garage space of 90,000 square feet. Land value is $1,300,000.00.

Cost of the proposed hypothetical project is calculated as follows:

Land costs (valuation): $1,300,000.00
Mortgage loan charges ($10,000,000.00): 50,000.00
Title costs: 3,000.00
Legal and accounting expenses: 8,000.00
Architect and engineering fees: 400,000.00
Soil tests: 7,000.00
Site preparation: 30,000.00
Contract cost estimate for building: 12,820,000.00
Furniture, equipment, and supplies: 10,000.00
Advertising and publicity: 17,000.00
Real estate commissions and promotional costs: 200,000.00
Interest, taxes, and insurance during construction: 130,000.00
Utility costs during construction: 10,000.00
Landscaping: 2,500.00
Incidental expenses: 5,000.00
Market and management survey: $12,500.00
Total final estimated cost for completed project: $15,005,000.00

**Note:** *All costs will vary from city to city as a result of differences in building code requirements, costs for materials and labor, climatic influences, local practices, etc.

## GROSS ANNUAL INCOME IS CALCULATED AS FOLLOWS:

| | |
|---|---|
| office space: 300,000 sq. ft. @ $7.00 | $2,100,000.00 |
| garage space: 300 spaces @ $360.00 | 108,000.00 |
| store space: 7,000 sq. ft. @ $12.00 | 84 000.00 |
| | ———————— |
| Gross per annum | $2,292,000.00 |

LESS: Allowance for vacancy and rent losses

-$ 142,000.00

ESTIMATED: annual gross effective income

$2,150,000.00

All of these calculations contemplate attractive architectural design; functional space layout; completely adequate facilities; full office building service, with all utilities except telephone included in rent; floor coverings; window shades and draperies; heat and air conditioning; and all major partitions, but excluding subpartitions.

The economics of the proposed hypothetical structure are tested by the following calculations:

Effective gross income after first year $2,150,000.00

Estimated expenses after first year:

| | |
|---|---|
| Taxes and licenses | $ 350,000.00 |
| Insurance | 12,000.00 |
| Management and administration | 75,000.00 |
| Building payroll and fringe benefits | 100,000.00 |
| Garage payroll and fringe benefits | 30,000.00 |
| Water, fuel, power and electricity | 31,000.00 |
| Elevator service and maintenance | 10,000.00 |
| Scavenger service | 3,000.00 |
| Contract services | |
| (landscaping, air conditioning, etc.) | 8,000.00 |
| Repairs and replacements | 16,000.00 |
| Painting and decorating | 10,000.00 |
| Supplies and sundries | 9,000.00 |
| Legal and auditing | 5,000.00 |
| Miscellaneous | 6,000.00 |

|  | 665,000.00 |
| Estimated effective net annual income | $1,485,000.00 |

Thus, on the estimated total cost of $15,000,000.00, the yield is approximately 10%. On the $5,000,000.00 equity, the yield becomes an estimated 13%, calculated as follows:

| Estimated effective net annual income | $1,485,000.00 |
| Less: | |
| Interest and reduction of principal on | $10,000,000.00 |
|  | 840 000.00 |
| Net cash available | $ 645,000.00 |

The above hypothetical calculations suggest an attractive, sound project deserving of a more intensive and detailed study prior to actual commitment. Local conditions must be carefully considered in arriving at final conclusions.

# OFFICE BUILDING CONSTRUCTION

We have now covered the general economic conditions that effect the office space market in the economy at large with its applications in one of our major centers of office use. Now we will study the practical problems confronting the builder, developer, or his agent in production of an office building. Under present economic conditions, it is very unwise to build a totally speculative office building. We therefore, find two types of buildings likely to start:

1.  Owner occupied usually institutional (insurance co., bank, major industrial center, etc.)
2.  Developer has core or key tenant who will occupy 30% to 60% of space.

# SITE SELECTION

The agent must first analyze the basic needs of the core tenant as to:

1.  Requirements (area and expansion)
2.  Budget
3.  Location (most important)

He must seek out a suitable site considering the following:

a.  geographical location (transportation, labor, etc.)
b.  available land and cost thereof
c.  permissive zoning (coverage, parking)

Even when there is no municipal requirement, most new buildings do provide parking. Increasing costs can cause quite a difference in square foot rental on a 100,000 sq. ft. building. A modified land residual technique can be used to assist in assessing land value.

# CONSTRUCTION CONTRACT

In considering the type of building there are four types of contract in general use:

1. Fixed Bid (lowest tender). This is inflexible and not always safe.
2. Cost Plus e.g., cost plus 10% for overhead and 10% profit. Weak, in that the more contractor spends, the more he makes.
3. Fixed Fee Plus Costs—some incentive to contractor to control costs.
4. Maximum Upset—guaranteed top with split savings on cost below the maximum to contractor to control costs.

These are general classifications. Today's contracts are usually complex and with highly competitive bidding they are often favorable to the owner.

# CONSTRUCTION TYPES

There are three popular types of construction:

1. Structural Steel—steel framework to the sky expensive, but a minimum of pillar space lost.
2. Reinforced Concrete—built floor by floor (cheaper, but more loss of space).
3. Left Slab—economical, but new and not yet perfected. Build floor at floor and lift them up.

**PARKING**—Most new buildings provide tenant and public needs.

**DESIGN**—There are many designs, but two basic ones are the following:

1.  Center Core is the best for rentability, has service in center and is best for light, splitting, maintaining, and renting.
2.  Side Core where adjacent building is cutting off light. Okay for long, narrow building, but on large area can create problems for dark areas, hard to rent. 10–12,000 sq. ft. is optimum per floor. Lighting 50 candle-power at desk level is desirable, some provide 70.

Partitioning can be treacherous-desirable to leave ceiling down until partitions are known-changes can put you in the poor house. It can cost $100.00 or more to move three fluorescent light fixtures one foot.

Generally, the wishes of the key tenant will dictate the design, and his budget will guide in the type and size of building.

The key tenant will control leasing terms on areas he has planned for expansion. Concessions will have to be made for shorter leases. Today's lease takeovers are a major problem for the owner. He must assess the recovery value on such leases. He must think of leasing commissions. In the following section we will discuss the methods adopted by the renter of space in satisfying clients seeking space. He may favor the building he knows, but must act for the user or lose a client in locating the proper space.

# PROMOTING THE NEW PROJECT

The initial success of a new office building depends largely on advance publicity plus an energetic, well-conceived leasing plan. However, particular restraint must be exercised in advance publicity to avoid extravagant promises that cannot be fulfilled; an attractive image of the completed project should embrace reality without any major exceptions.

Preconstruction public notice should not excessively precede the date on which construction actually start, lest the public will lose interest and the time, energy and expense for publicity be expended needlessly. Initial publicity should contain an architectural rendering supported by an identification of the neighborhood and a listing of the facilities and services that will definitely be available. A fair approximation of the completion date is essential, since it stimulates advance planning by prospective tenants and can be effectively tied to the leasing program.

Advance promotion is handled primarily through press releases, closely followed by the brochure and lease data portfolio. There are many theories concerning the extensiveness, or brevity of the lease data portfolio. It is the author's contention that the more complete the portfolio, the more effective the leasing program will be. Such a brochure portfolio should contain:

- A sketch of the building in true relationship to its neighborhood
- A statement about services and facilities that will be available, and at whose cost
- A correct approximation of the total usable rental space per floor
- A typical floor plan to a stated scale
- At least one sample office layout to scale
- Name, address, and telephone number of the leasing and management agent

If some advance leases have been made to prestige tenants, this also should be stated. Some developers believe that the leasing brochure should even go so far as to state the rental ranges for various office areas. It is the author's opinion that in many instances, this may avoid time lost in negotiation and may correct erroneous estimates made by prospective tenants that might otherwise confuse the leasing program.

Wherever the situation justifies, the leasing portfolio may be supplemented by a descriptive folder publicizing the new building and designed for broader distribution. As in all advertising programs, continuing newspaper coverage, paid or gratis, is essential to keeping public interest alive.

# COMMERCIAL REAL ESTATE
## SESSION No. TWO
## THE OFFICE BUILDING

## THE TENANT'S VIEWPOINT

## THE MARKET FOR OFFICE SPACE

The market for office space is a dynamic force affected by many influences, a large number of which are detected only through the eyes and ears of the inexperienced professional. Supply and demand factors and the nature of competition are the obvious economic weather vanes which must be carefully and continuously studied; in each of these, the direction of the trend is more significant than the current status.

The market for office space must be studied in small segments. Overall statistics for the office space market will not give a true picture for a specific property. Buildings should be grouped as to age, condition, location, facilities, and amenities. That overall market date can be dangerously misleading, is apparent in the observation that "average" vacancy is 10% at the same time that vacancy in new buildings is 2% or less. This means that vacancies up to 16% or 20% can exist in older buildings.

In the case of an older building with some curable obsolescence and deferred maintenance, management must determine the available supply of space in comparable buildings. It must also assess trends in occupancy for this general building classification in the neighborhood of the subject property. If the supply of space appears to be increasing, management should be encouraged to embark on some immediate constructive planning to upgrade the entire building. If the supply of space is decreasing, it is probable that management can come fairly close to retaining the status quo of normal occupancy.

In the case of an older building, management should also study the movements of tenants from older to newer buildings to analyze the potential for increased future use of the older property. Many times it will be noted that the space vacated by tenants moving in new buildings is absorbed by tenants who have determined that they receive few or no benefits from the more modern and comparatively expensive space. This is generally true of tenants who have little contact with the public and whose principal specification is location and layout. Once the demand pattern is established, the rental program becomes clear-cut as to types of tenancies, rent charges, services, facilities, and modernization and other capital improvements.

The availability of off-street parking close at hand often becomes a strong factor in the demand for space in central office buildings. In most cases, the requirements for parking are related more to organization personnel than to the public. It is this situation that has caused parking-to office space ratios to creep into the zoning and building ordinances of many of the larger communities.

It is important to keep in mind that the availability of desirable office space can, in itself, create an effective demand. The factors affecting demand include: expansion and retraction of space needs by existing tenancies; new local businesses and tenant going out of the community and movement into the community. All of these factors must be carefully appraised to determine the net effect on total available space.

Currently the demand for office space in the more populated cities is on the increase and will continue in that direction for the foreseeable future. However, this does not mean that all available space will be quickly absorbed. Every community has its own rate of space absorption; therefore, the professional must familiarize himself with this rate based upon recent history of office building use and weigh it carefully against probable supply.

# OFFICE RENTALS

The renting or leasing of office space is highly specialized and lucrative field of endeavor. The well-organized office will keep an up to date inventory of available space.

When preparing a list for a specific client, a selection is made from inventory. This, of course, contains more detail after it has been established that the client wishes to locate in a certain area.

The trained renter of office space is familiar with office routines and procedures for all businesses. To be successful, he must appeal to the needs of the client and sell him on a particular area ideal for him.

The following outline is designed to show some of the questions that bother the would-be tenant. It is the task of the agent to answer these questions capable, having determined which are the most important to the individual client.

1. First and foremost is location. Is it convenient for:
   a. the tenant, his clients, and employees?
   b. banks and restaurants?
   c. all forms of transportation?

2. Make-up of the building
   a. will he be proud to be their neighbor?
   b. are some customers or prospective customers now tenants?
   c. is the ownership sound and substantial?
   d. is management known for good service and fair dealing?
   e. do owners have one price policy or questionable deals?

3. Layout of the space
    a. plan with every foot usable
    b. best work flow with no waste promotion
    c. price per sq. ft. not as important as layout

In some buildings tenants need 125 sq. ft., per employee; and it can be as low in typing and accounting pools as 75 sq. ft.

In one building, as a result of layout a tenant may need 100 sq. ft. per employee at $4.50 per square foot.

In another, he might require 90 sq. ft. per employee at $5.00 per sq. ft.

In each case, the costs is $450.00 per year, per employee. But since it has improved layout efficiency, the second building will no doubt be more modern and better equipped.

4. Service
    a. is sufficient parking space provided?
    b. spic and span—well decorated—good repair?
    c. are toilets, lights, clean—well maintained and well located?
    d. can elevators handle peaks?
    e. comfortable heat and air conditioning?
    f. is the staff polite and capable?

5. Advertising value
    a. prestige
    b. size
    c. architecture
    d. address, floodlighting, etc.
    e. glamorous and functional lobby

6. Leasing terms
    a. partitioning
    b. parking concessions
    c. length of lease

    d.   renewal privilege
    e.   escalator clause
    f.   rates
    g.   cost of relocation

# THE RENTAL PROGRAM

Experience and training encourage the professional to give first consideration to the gross income stream. Rental planning calls for many studies, all of which should help to determine the maximum income available with stability. Thus, the market analysis should completely bracket the rentals which might reasonably be expected from desirable tenants.

## Setting the rent schedule

A uniform rent schedule is essential to sound management. Such a schedule must reflect all of those factors which tenants customarily consider part of rental value. These include: height above the street level, location on floor as related to elevator accessibility, outlook and natural light.

All of the various formulas that have been developed for establishing a rent schedule are based on a typical space that is classified as 100%, with the remaining spaces graded up or down, depending on enhances or reduced desirability. As in most real estate matters, the successful use of formulas relies on the quality of the realtor's judgment. Often a testing of the market will suggest alterations or changes in the application of any adopted formula.

Once an equitable and realistic rent schedule has been established, it should be rigidly adhered to if the tenant's goodwill and confidence are to be maintained. In almost all cases of haphazard rent pricing, the buildings have suffered financially.

# LEASING PRACTICES

Proven renting practices require scale floor plans and a series of office layouts for various floor areas that will permit the prospective tenant to study his particular layout problem in the fight of alternatives that are being used by others. The realtor must acquaint himself with needs of the prospect by visiting the prospects' current office (if feasible), by studying his problems and needs, and by actually preparing suggested office layouts showing subspace sizes and location of office furniture, equipment and facilities. Although it has become general practice for tenants to pay for subpartitioning, the realtor should work closely with the tenant, or his architect, to insure the best use of the space within the limits of the structure and its facilities.

In the early stages of negotiation, the prospective tenant should receive a sample of the standard lease form used in the building. While local laws and customs will dictate the general lease clauses and some of the special clauses, modern building operation suggests additional special clauses: provisions for controlling the use of common areas and facilities, agreements in the events of expropriation and escalator clauses protect the owner against rising costs resulting primarily from increased labor costs, and ad valorem real estate taxes. In lease for terms beyond five years, it is often advisable to include some provision for rent adjustment to compensate for changes in the cost of living, or in some acceptable regularly published index. The basic lease should be prepared by competent legal counsel, and any special clauses should have the benefit of expert legal advice.

# MEASUREMENT OF FLOOR SPACE

The recommended standard method of floor measurement for office buildings is that prescribed by the National Association of Building Owners and Managers.

## NET RENTABLE AREA

The net rentable area of a multiple tenant's floor shall be the sum of all rentable areas on that floor. The rentable area of an office on a multiple tenancy floor shall be computed by measuring to the inside finish of permanent outer building walls, to the office side of the corridors and/or other permanent partitions, and to the center of partitions that separate the premises from adjoining rentable areas.

No deductions shall be made for columns and projections necessary to the building.

## FULL FLOOR RENTABLE AREA

The rentable area of a single tenancy floor shall be computed by measuring to the inside finish of permanent building walls. Rentable area of a single tenancy floor shall include all area within outside walls, less stairs, elevator shafts, flues, stack, pipe shafts, and vertical duets with their enclosing walls. Toilets, air conditioning rooms, fan rooms, janitor's closets and electrical closets within, and exclusively serving only that floor, shall be included in rentable area.

No deductions shall be made for columns and projections necessary to the building.

## TENANT SELECTION

The tenant roster of the average central city office building will include attorneys, accountants, architects, engineers, corporate business offices, insurance organizations, stock and bond brokers, real estate offices, and investment companies, and a fairly large group of smaller tenancies of a general business or investment nature. Many of the larger buildings will lease space for barbershop facilities at substantial discounts and an added convenience to tenants. Those buildings which cater to large groups of attorneys usually maintain a law library for their use. In some buildings, substantial areas will be leased to governmental agencies which do business with business people.

It is essential that leasing practices contemplate adequate opportunity for expansion by major tenants. This is best accomplished by short leases for tenants with smaller space, who can easily be moved to other locations in the building. Allocation of excessively larger spaces to even the best tenants should be avoided on relatively long leases (in excess of ten years); vacating of large spaces can create serious rent losses and expensive renovation. By the same token, very short leases, even for small tenants can result in excessive tenant turnover, which also is costly. The best practice under ordinary conditions is to require leases on all space and to avoid month-to-month occupancies.

Tenant selection is basic to the creation of prestige. Therefore, qualifying the tenant is a management responsibility that must be pursued diligently. The well-known national organization presents no problems, but the smaller business and professional prospect must be carefully screened as to financial responsibility and reputation. Over anxiety to rent the space at any cost can result in a downgrading of the property and in unfortunate credit losses.

# THE BUILDING MANAGER

The building manager must be:

1.  A keen business man.
2.  A first-class auditor.
3.  A student of the business that he wants as tenants.
4.  A shrewd purchasing agent.
5.  An intelligent record keeper and analyzer.
6.  A draftsman to layout offices.
7.  A construction superintendent.
8.  A lawyer—enough to handle leases and contracts.
9.  On good terms with officials and lawmakers.

10. Able to understand and practice good employee, tenant, and public relations.

The following will show how the manager of a modern office building is required to exhibit the above abilities:

A.  His responsibilities in the operation of the building—including all kinds of mechanical equipment. Formerly 20% of operating cost of a building was mechanical, but now that figure is 40% because of additional mechanization.

  On the average there will be one operating employee for every 3,000 square feet of office space.

B.  Income Production—office buildings have high capital investment.

Its costs are high and for each dollar of income, the following could be typical costs:

| Fixed charges, insurance, taxes, and depreciation | .26 |
| Wages | .27 |
| 6% return on investment | <u>.28</u> |
| | .81 |

Therefore, an office building as stated earlier, has to be over 80% rented to carry itself. Until that level is reached, a new building operates at a loss. The building manager must provide for the income and its expenditure.

C.  Legislative Field—includes broadly: taxes, building codes and regulations. In most cities, office buildings pay 10–15% of the taxes. Managers and their associations feel that the taxes are often excessive and appeals are frequent.

# CONCLUSIONS AND THE FUTURE

The central city is here to stay. The current office building boom reflects confidence in the future of the city. Those well qualified judges of the future that back their opinions with millions of dollars favor the city. The leading institutions, builders, and promoters have all agreed, but the decision was made for them by the law of supply and demand. Users of office space have demanded expansion of the city and the supply is being provided.

# OFFICE BUILDING

Only in the city can the chairman of the board walk to his club for lunch and discuss business with his associates and competitors.

Only in the city can the vital female clerical staff have the glamour of the city shops, offices and variety of activities.

Only in the city do major traffic arteries provide mass movement to the great office complex.

The physical future is in the hands of the inventors, engineers, and scientists. Possibly the jet age, the interspace age, and the electronic age will change everything. Some of the new developments to be noted are:

a. The growing use of computers and data processing and their effect of office location building design, hours of work, etc.

b. High speed elevators, underground parking, fluorescent ceiling lighting, and other special features of new buildings accelerate the obsolescence of relatively newer buildings which do not have these features.

c. Trend toward leasing instead of ownership.

d. Increased size of office buildings.

e. The development of chain ownership of office buildings.

A new generation of trained planners, architects and realtors with knowledge and skill will influence the future disposition of our real property. It will be their duty to apply the new techniques within the framework of the all-controlling law of supply and demand.

NOTE: In the foregoing narrative, some figures have been quoted. It must be clearly understood that these are quoted in the hope that they will serve as guides to an understanding of the particular problems to which they have been applied. These rules of thumb and typical figures are subject to justifiable criticism and question by everyone concerned with building, management or leasing. Their use on any specific property is not defensible and they are intended to serve as hypothetical guide posts.

# Section Three
# FOREIGN INVESTORS IN
# UNITED STATES REAL ESTATE

This chapter is designed to provide a general understanding of the United States income tax effects on foreign investors from their operation and disposition of United States real estate and real property interests. Particular attention is paid to the tax consequences to foreign investors upon their disposition of United States real estate or ownership interests in certain entities which hold United States real estate.

This chapter begins by briefly discussing the basic income tax provisions which impact a foreign investor which owns or operates United States real property. The chapter continues by discussing the Foreign Investment in Real Property Tax Act of 1980 (FIRPTA), the basic taxation provisions thereof and the intricate withholding system for the enforcement of FIRPTA. The chapter concludes with a discussion of additional taxes imposed on foreign corporations which have a branch in the United States and the interplay of these branch level taxes with United States income tax treaties.

HERMAN R. WILLIAMS

# Taxation on Income Not Connected With United States Trade or Business

In general, a foreign person is subject to a 30% tax on certain gross income received from sources within the United States to the extent such amounts are not effectively connected with the conduct of a trade or business within the United States. Such income is taxed in the gross basis without any deductions or allowances. The 30% tax is imposed on amounts received from sources within the United States as interests, dividends, rents, salaries, wages, premiums, annuities, compensation on and other fixed or determinable annual or periodic gains, profits, and income. Unless effectively connected with conduct of a trade or business within the United States, income of the nature includes, inter alia:

(1) All rental income from real estate within the United States; (2) Stated rental income plus any other payments made by a lessee on net leased property located within the United States; (3) Dividends paid by a foreign corporation if, and to the extent that, 25% or more of its gross income from all sources is effectively connected with the conduct of a trade or business within the United States; (4) Dividends paid by a United States corporation; and (5) Interest paid by a United States corporation unless more than 80% of its gross income is from sources outside the United States.

A nonresident alien present in the United States for a period of, or periods aggregating, 183 days or more during the taxable year, is subject to a 30% tax on the amounts by which his capital gains, derived from sources within the United States, exceed his capital losses, allocable to sources within the United States, from sales or exchanges of capital assets during the taxable year. However, a foreign person's gain or loss from the disposition of United States real property interests is subject to tax under Section 897, and is treated as effectively connected with the conduct of a trade or business within the United States without regard to this physical presence test.

# Taxation on Income Connected With United States Trade or Business

A foreign person engaged in trade or business within the United States during the taxable year is taxable, to the extent such person's taxable income is effectively connected with the conduct of such trade or business, on a net income basis in a manner similar to the taxation of United States persons. A foreign person may desire to have his United States activities characterized as being effectively connected with a trade or business within the United States so as to be taxed on a net basis rather than a gross basis. Net basis taxation applies only to the taxable income of a foreign person that is effectively connected with the conduct of a trade or business within the United States.

If a foreign person is engaged in the conduct of a trade or business within the United States and also has United States source income which is not effectively connected with the person's trade or business, such noneffectively connected income is taxed on the gross amount at the 30% rate.

A foreign person may elect, with respect to his income derived from United States real estate activities, regardless of whether such activities constitute a trade or business, to be taxed as if such income were effectively connected with the conduct of a trade or business within the United States. Where such election is made, a foreign person will be taxed on a net basis with respect to income derived from real property located within the United States.

Thus, whether a foreign person is subject to United States income taxation on a gross basis or a net basis depends on whether such income is effectively connected with the conduct of a trade or business within the United States. If the foreign investor in United States real estate does not elect to have the income from such investment treated as income effectively connected with the conduct of a trade or business within the United States, it may be unclear whether the foreign person is engaged in the conduct of a trade or business within the United States by his ownership of United States real property.

In general, the mere ownership of United States real property by a foreign person, without more, does not constitute the conduct of a trade or business within the United States. However, if a foreign person's activities extend beyond the mere ownership of the property and collection of the rents therefrom, so that the foreign person's activities are viewed considerable, continuous and regular, the person will be characterized as engaged in the conduct of a trade or business within the United States. For the purpose of making this determination, activities conducted by an agent for a foreign person will be attributable to the foreign person.

If a single piece of United States real property is net leased, the foreign owner generally will not be considered to be engaged in the conduct of a trade or business within the United States. On the other hand, the leasing number of United States real properties may in and of itself constitute the conduct of a trade or business in the United States. Where a lease is not a true net lease, a foreign person may avoid being characterized as engaged in the conduct of a trade or business in the United States. For example, the service has rules that a foreign lessor owning United States real property subject to a lease was not engaged in the conduct of a trade or business within the United States though was not lease provided both that (1) the lessor would pay the real property taxes and insurance and (2) the lessor would receive additional rent based upon lessee's gross income.

In addition, a foreign person may not be considered engaged in the conduct of a United States trade or business if the entire property is net leased to an intermediary such as a management company.

If United States property owned by a foreign person is not net leased, then management of the property by the foreign person or his agent will generally cause the foreign person to be considered engaged in the conduct of a trade or business within the United States.

Foreign persons may prefer to have their United States real estate activities treated as a United States trade or business because they will be taxed on a net basis, rather than on their gross income from such activities. If a foreign person is taxed on net income, the foreign person may generally compute his taxable income by offsetting his effectively gross income with all available deductions to the extent that such deductions are effectively connected with the conduct of such United States trade or business.

In any event, foreign persons can only obtain the benefit of the various deductions and tax credits by filing a United States income tax return. The income tax deductions and credits applicable with respect to real estate are more fully discussed elsewhere in the text.

## Election to Treat Real Property Income as Effectively Connected

The code and most United States income tax provide that a foreign person may elect to treat income derived from United States real property as effectively connected with the conduct of a trade or business within the United States and thereby subject such income to taxation in a net basis, regardless of whether the foreign person is engaged in the conduct of a United States trade or business or whether such person's income is effectively connected with such United States trade or business. The election applies to all United States real property owned by a foreign person and all of the income from such property, including gain from the sale thereof. Most treaties also so provide. However, each treaty must be carefully read to determine its exact scope.

The code election (and similar treaty elections) applies not only to rental income, but also to royalties from mines, wells and other material resources, and to gains from certain sales of timber, coal and iron ore. If for the taxable year the taxpayer has no income from United States real property, or from any interest in such real property, the code election may not be made. However, where an election has been properly made for a particular taxable year, the election remains in effect, unless properly revoked, for subsequent taxable years despite the fact that the tax payer has no income from real property, or an interest therein, to which the election applies.

The code election does not apply to the interest from a debt obligation secured by a mortgage on real property, dividends from real estate investment trusts, rentals from property not held for the production of income from any transaction in such property not entered into for profit, royalties from intangible personal property, or income that is considered effectively connected with the conduct of a United States trade or business without regard to the code election.

It is important to realize that the making of the code election does not cause a foreign person to be considered engaged in the conduct of a trade or business within the United States. Rather, the election causes the foreign person's other items of income and deduction attributable to United States real property to be considered as income which is effectively connected with the conduct of a trade or business within the United States. A foreign person's other items of income and deduction that are generated from the United States sources do not become effectively connected by reason of this election.

According to the regulations, deductions in excess of income will not result in a net operating loss carry-over where the code election is in effect. This result to contrary in language contained in the Conference Report accompanying the Foreign Investment in Real Property Tax Act of 1980. That language states that "Losses attributable to the United States real property from prior to the year of sale would be allowed as deductions against the foreign investor's effectively connected United States gross income (including gains from real property sales) if the foreign investor elects under section 871 (d) or 882 (d) to be taxable on a net basis on its United States real property investment income."

Once made, the code election is irrevocable unless the service consents to revocation. However, the code election can be revoked without the service's consent where the period of limitations on credits or refunds for the taxable year in which the election was made has not expired.

While the code election is generally irrevocable, many treaty elections are annual elections. This allows a foreign person the flexibility to choose annually the basis, gross or net, by which his income attribute to United States real property will be taxed. Foreign investors making this election pursuant to a treaty, rather than under the code, must carefully read the treaty both to determine its scope and to discover the requirements which must be met in order to qualify for the election, because treaties may vary with respect to these issues.

# General Rules of FIRPTA

Prior to Foreign Investment in Real Property Tax Act of 1980 (FIRPTA), nonresident alien individuals and foreign corporations were generally not subject to United States income tax on gains realized from the sale, or other disposition of United States real estate unless those gains were attributable to the conduct of a trade or business within the United States, or in the case of a nonresident alien individual, unless he or she was present in the United States for 183 days of more during the year that the gain was realized. According to a foreign person could minimize, or even eliminate, his United States income tax by structuring his activities so as to avoid being engaged in a trade or business within the United States. Moreover, there were several techniques available to a foreign investor who was engaged in a United States trade or business to wholly avoid United States tax on the gain from the sale of United States real estate. It was the avoidance of tax that concerned congress and prompted it to enact FIRPTA.

FIRPTA addresses this congressional concern by providing that the gain or loss of a nonresident alien or a foreign corporation from the disposition of a United States real property interest is treated as if such trade or business during the year and as if such gain or loss were effectively connected with such trade or business. Thus, foreign person will generally be subject to United States income tax on the sale or disposition of their United States real estate.

For disposition occurring after December 31,1986, the least amount of FIRPTA tax imposed upon nonresident alien individuals is equal to least 21% of the lesser of the individual's alternative minimum taxable income for the taxable year or the individual's net United States real property gain for the taxable year. An individual's net United States real property gain for a taxable year is equal to the excess of (1) the individual's aggregate gains over (2) the individual's aggregate losses from dispositions of United States real property interests. Nonresident alien individuals are the same except that the applicable rate of tax is 20%.

Foreign corporations having FIRPTA gains are taxed the same as United States corporations. In other words, foreign corporations are subject to the regular corporate income tax, the corporate alternative minimum tax and the alternative tax for corporations.

Significant FIRPTA Definitions and Operating Rules

The key to understanding FIRPTA, as well as to minimizing the adverse tax consequences which FIRPTA can create, lies in understanding both the broadly defined terms central to FIRPTA's general rule and the complex "look through" and attribution rules which make it difficult for a foreign investor to avoid FIRPTA by holding United States real property indirectly through various entities.

# Taxpayers Subject to FIRPTA

By its terms, FIRPTA applies to nonresident alien individuals and foreign corporations. A nonresident alien individual, for purposes of United States tax laws, is an individual who is neither a citizen nor a resident of the United States. An alien individual is treated as a United States resident if he neither is a lawful permanent resident of the United States, or meets the substantial presence test. An individual is considered to be a lawful permanent resident of the United States if at any time he is of the status of having been lawfully accorded the privilege of residing permanently in the United States as an immigrant in accordance with the immigration laws and such status has neither been revoked nor abandoned, such abandonment having been determined administratively or judicially.

An alien individual meets the substantial presence test, and is thus considered a residence alien for the taxable year, if he was both present in the United States for at least thirty-one days during the calendar year and the sum of (1) the number of days the individual was physically present during the current calendar, plus (2) one-third of the number of days the individual was physically present in the

United States during the immediately preceding calendar year, (3) one-sixth of the number of says the individual was physically in the United States during the second preceding calendar year equals or exceed 183 days. An individual who otherwise satisfies the substantial presence test will not be considered a resident alien if such individual is physically present in the United States on less than 183 days during the current calendar year, and for such year, the individual both has a tax home in a foreign country and has a closer connection to such foreign country than to the United States.

Foreign corporations are also subject to FIRPTA. By definition, a foreign corporation is a corporation which is neither created nor organized in the United States or under the law of the United States or of any states. This definition has been strictly applied to exclude corporations organized under the laws of the United States possession.

## US Real Property Interests

FIRPTA's characterization of the gain or loss from the disposition of United States real estate as effectively connected with the conduct of a United States trade or business applies only to the disposition of a United States real property interest (USRPI). A USRPI can be held by a foreign person either directly as an interest in real property located in the United States or the Virgin Islands, or through an entity such as a partnership, trust or estate, or as an interest in a domestic corporation.

In order for an interest in a domestic corporation to be classified as a USRPI, the corporation must be a United States real property holding corporation (USRPHC) and the interest must be characterized as other than an interest solely as a creditor.

# Interest in Real Property

An interest in real property is broadly defined to include free ownership and co-ownership of land or improvements thereon, leaseholds of land or improvements thereon, option to acquire land or improvements thereon. An improvement on real property, for the purpose of FIRPTA is a building; any other inherently permanent structure, and the structural components of each.

The term real property also includes such tangible personal property as movable walls, furnishings and other personality associated with the use of real property. Personal property is associated with the use of real property only if it is predominantly used to exploit unsurveyed natural products in or upon the land, if is predominantly used to construct or otherwise carry out improvements to real property; if it is predominantly used in connection with the operation of a lodging facility; or if it is predominantly used by a lessor to provide furnished office or other work space to lessees.

Personal property that has become associated with the use of a real property interest is itself treated as a real property interest upon disposition, unless either the personal property is disposed of more than one year before the disposition of any present right to used or occupy the real property with which it was associated, or the personal property is disposed of more than one year after the disposition of all present rights to use or occupy the real property with which it was associated, or the personal property and the real property with which it was associated are separately sold to persons that are related neither to the transferor nor one another.

# Interest Other than Interest Solely as Creditor

The term "USRPI" includes any interest in United States real property, other than an interest which is solely that of a creditor, whether held directly or held through any domestic corporation or other entity. An interest in real property other than an interest solely as a creditor includes a free ownership, co-ownership or leasehold interest, a time sharing interest, and a life estate, remainder or reversionary interest in real property.

A person, both individual and corporate, is considered to hold an interest in real property other than that of a creditor if such person has any right, directly or indirectly, to share in the appreciation in the value of, or in the gross or net profits generated by, the real property.

Example 1. Assume that a nonresident alien individual lends a United States citizen funds to purchase a parcel of real property located in the United States. Further, assume that under the terms of the loan the interest payments due on the note are determined according to the gross proceeds generated by the property, as well as by the property's appreciation in value. Since the nonresident alien individual has a right to share in the gross proceeds generated by the property, as well as in the property's appreciation in value, such individual will be treated as holding a USRPI because such loan is an interest in real property other than a pure creditor's interest.

Although the creditor in the above example is considered to be holding a USRPI, the general rule of FIRPTA will not apply to the creditor's collection of principal and interest payments on the debt, assuming the debt is treated as debt for tax purposes because the collection of principal and interest payments do not constitute gain within the meaning of Section 1001. However, if the note were sold by the foreign person prior to maturity, the resulting gain, if any, would be subject to taxation under FIRPTA.

The regulations under FIRPTA provide detailed guidance as to whether certain types of creditors' interests will constitute an interest solely as a creditor of real property. These regulations provide similar rules with regard to whether an interest in an entity will be considered an interest solely as a creditor.

# United States Real Property Holding Corporations

As previously noted, the concept of the USRPI encompasses any interest in a USRPI. A corporation is a USRPHC if the fair market value of its USRPIs, of any applicable determination date, equals or exceeds 50% of the sum of the fair market value of its USRPIs, its interests in real property located outside the United States, and any other assets which are used or held for use in a trade or business.

If a corporation qualifies as a USRPHC on any applicable determination date after June 18, 1980, any interest in such corporation will generally be treated as a USRPI for five-year period from such date. The taxpayer has the burden of establishing that a corporation is not a USRPHC. In order to avoid both USRPHC status and to simplify the burden of demonstrating non-USRPHC status, a foreign-controlled United States operating company, with other than a real estate related business, should avoid acquiring an ownership interest in its office space and should lease such space at a fair market value rental.

The space should be leased from either an unrelated party or a sister company formed to own such real estate. By having the sister corporation hold and lease the United States real property to the operating corporation, the foreign investor will be able to invest in the United States real estate. Through a lease, the foreign investor can use such United States real estate in the trade or business of the operating company, and minimize the potential for the operating company to be characterized as a USRPHC.

A corporation is tested for treatment as a USRPHC on four applicable determination dates. These dates are:

1. The last day of the corporation's taxable year
2. The date on which the corporation acquires any USRPI
3. The date on which the corporation disposes of an interest in real property located outside the United States or disposes of other assets used or held for use in a trade or business during the calendar year

4. For a corporation which is considered constructively to own a portion of the assets of another entity, the date when such entity either acquires a USRPI, disposes of an interest in real property located in United States or disposes of other assets used or held for use as a trade or business during the calendar year

In making a determination as to whether a corporation is a USRPHC, the taxpayer is required, for purposes of the 50% test, to include:

1. USRPIs held directly by the corporation
2. Interests in real property located outside the United States held by the corporation
3. Assets used or held for use in a trade or business that are held directly by the corporation
4. A proportionate share of assets held through a partnership, trust or estate
5. A proportionate share of assets held through a domestic or foreign corporation in which the corporations holds a controlling interest

An interest held by the domestic corporation in a foreign corporation is also considered to be a USRPI for purposes of determining whether the domestic corporation is a USRPHC, unless the taxpayer proves otherwise. However, regardless of whether an interest in foreign corporation is a USRPI for this purpose, gain or loss from the disposition of an interest in such foreign corporation will not be treated as effectively connected with a United States trade or business under Section 897(a). In addition, a corporation which is a holder of an interest in a partnership, trust or estate is considered to hold a proportionate share of the assets held by such entity.

As noted above, in determining whether a corporation is a USRPHC, the taxpayer must include a proportionate share of the assets held by the foreign or domestic corporation in which the corporation holds a controlling interest. A controlling interest constitutes 50% or more of the fair market value of all classes of stock of the corporation. For these purposes, the attribute rules of Section 318 (a) apply, except that attribution both to and from corporations occurs at a 5%, rather than 50%, ownership level.

# Interests Excepted from USRPI Classification

Certain interests are statutorily or administratively excepted from USRPI status. Where a class of corporate stock is regularly traded on an established securities market, an interest in such stock will generally not be treated as a USRPI unless the person disposing of the stock owned more than 5% of the fair market value of that class of stock during the five-year period ending on either the date of disposition of such stock or another applicable determination date.

For purposes of determining whether a person's ownership exceeds 5%, the attribution rules of Section 318(a) apply, except that attribution to and from corporations occurs at a 5%, rather than 50%, ownership level.

A USRPI does not include an interest in a corporation (a former USRPHC) which has disposed of all of its USRPIS in transactions in which the full amount of gain, if any, was recognized.

Finally, an interest in a domestically controlled REIT is not a USRPI. A domestically controlled REIT is one in which less than 50% of the fair market value of the outstanding stock was directly or in directly held by foreign persons during five-year period ending on the applicable determination date.

# Other FIRPTA Provisions

This section provides a summary of several additional FIRPTA provisions, regarding the application of FIRPTA to specific situations and transactions.

FIRPTA applies to a foreign corporation upon its distribution of a USRPI. A foreign corporation must recognize gain upon its distribution of a USRPI to the extent that the fair market value of the USRPI exceeds the adjusted basis therein. The general rule applies regardless of whether the distribution was made as an ongoing distribution, a liquidating distribution, or as a distribution in redemption of a stockholder's shares.

However, this rule does not apply where, at the time of the distribution, the distributee would be subject to United States taxation on a subsequent disposition of the distributed property and the basis of the distributed property in the hands of the distributee is no greater than the adjusted basis before the distribution as increased by the amount of gain recognized by the distributing corporation.

In general, gain on the distribution of a USRPI also is not recognized by a distributing foreign corporation in complete liquidation of its subsidiary. Detailed regulations exist under Section 897(d) and (e) providing for gain limitations provisions in connection with distributions of USRPIS by foreign corporations.

In general, any nonrecognition provision of the code applies to the exchange of a USRPI only if the sale of the property received in such transaction would be subject to United States tax. If a nonrecognition provision does not apply, the USRPI transferred is subject to taxation under FIRPTA. The service has also issued regulations addressing the applicability of nonrecognition provisions to, inter alia, the transfer of a USRPI in a Section 355 distribution and the sale of a nonresident alien's principle residence.

The service has ruled previously that where a foreign corporation exchanges one USRPI for another USRPI in a Section 351(a) tax-free incorporation, the nonrecognition provisions of Section 351 will apply for purposes of FIRPTA, so long as the foreign corporation's sale of the second USRPI will clearly be subject to United States taxation.

However, the service will deny nonrecognition in certain tax avoidance transactions, including certain transfers by foreign persons to domestic corporations, certain related person transactions, and certain plans that rearrange the incidents of ownership of a USRPI to gain treaty benefits. FIRPTA also applies to domestic corporations upon its distribution of a USRPI to either a nonresident alien individual or a foreign corporation. If such basis a distribution is made by such a corporation with respect to its stock, then the basis of the distributed USRPI to the foreign distributee cannot exceed the adjusted basis of such property to the distributing corporation, increased by the gain recognized by such corporation on the distribution and any United States taxes paid by the foreign distributee on the distribution. This provision reflects the congressional intent to prevent foreign real estate investors from receiving a stepped up basis for their investments in United States real estate in situations either where no income tax has been paid or where the amount of income tax owed has been reduced by treaty.

FIRPTA also applies to sales of interest in partnerships, trusts and estates such that the amount of any consideration received by a foreign person in exchange for all or part of its interest in a partnership, trust or estate is, to the extent attributable to a USRPI, considered as an amount received from the sale or exchange in the United States of such property.

FIRPTA is also applicable to nondomestically controlled REITs. A nondomestically controlled REIT is one which 50% or more of the fair market value of the outstanding stock was held by foreign persons during five-year period ending on a particular determination date.

FIRPTA rules also allow certain foreign corporations to be treated as domestic corporations. Under Section 897 (i), a foreign corporation that holds a USRPI is entitled to nondiscriminatory tax treatment under a United States treaty obligation, and upon making proper election, it will be treated as a domestic corporation for purposes of FIRPTA and the withholding rules.

In order to properly make such election, all of the owners of all classes of interests (other than interest held solely as a creditor) must, at the time of the election, consent to the making of the election and agree that any gain from the disposition of a USRPI will be taxable irrespective of any contrary treaty provisions to which the United States is a party.

A foreign corporation permitted to make this election may do so at any time before the first transaction which would be subject to FIRPTA in the absence of this election. The period to which the election applies begins on the date upon which the election is made, or on such earlier date as is set forth in the election, but not earlier than June 19, 1980. If not revoked, this election can only be revoked with the permission of the Treasury.

Finally, note that certain corporations otherwise eligible to elect to be treated as domestic corporations may make such elections only if they comply with the service's antiabuse rule. Taxpayers subject to FIRPTA are required to recognize gain on the transfer of a USRPI to a foreign corporation if the transfer is made as a capital contribution or as paid in surplus. This provision prevents foreigners from avoiding FIRPTA by transferring a USRPI to a corporation in a transaction structured as a nonrecognition transaction.

The amount of gain required to be recognized upon such transfer is the excess of the fair market value of the property transferred over the sum of the transferor's adjusted basis and the amount of any gain otherwise recognized to the transfer or at the time of the transfer.

# FIRPTA Withholding Requirements
## General Rule

To collect taxes due pursuant to FIRPTA, congress enacted withholding requirements under code Section 1445. Section 1445 requires the transferee of a USRPI to deduct and withhold from the transferor, and pay over to the service, a tax equal to 10% of the amount realized by the transferor on the disposition. Transactions falling within FIRPTA which occur on or after January 1, 1985, are subject to such withholding. Neither the transferee's duty to withhold nor the amount required to be withheld is affected by the amount of cash to be paid by the transferee.

However, the transferor must have an amount realized for the withholding rules to apply. Thus, where the amount realized by the transferor is zero—for example, where the transferor transfer a USRPI as a gift to the transferee, who furnishes no consideration to the transferor and assumes no liabilities of the transferor-withholding by the transferee is not required. In a situation where the USRPI is jointly owned by foreign and nonforeign transferors, the amount which the transferee is required to withhold is determined by allocating the amount realized to the transferors based upon the capital contributions of each transferors with respect to the property. Example 1. Assume that a parcel of real property located within the United States is owned jointly by a United States citizen and a nonresident alien individual. When these joint owners purchased the property, assume that each joint owner paid 50% of the down payment on the note used to finance the acquisition. Also, one-half of all debt service payments have been made by each person. If the property is sold for $500,000, the transferee is required to deduct and withhold from the transferor, and pay over to the service, $25,000 (10% of the amount realized allocated to the foreign transferor, which is $250,000).

The service generally requires that the transferor must report and pay over any tax withheld by the twentieth day after the date of transfer. An exception is made for transferees who have applied for withholding certificates. In general, a withholding certificate is a certificate issued by the service that either excuses the transferee from the withholding requirements or permits the transferee to adjust the amount required to be withheld.

Where the transferee of a USRPI has an application for a withholding certificate pending with the service, any tax withheld by the transferee must be paid over within twenty days after the service's final determination (to the extent required) as to such application. In general, every person required to deduct and withhold tax under FIRPTA is liable for the payment of that tax. Thus, a person required to deduct and withhold the FIRPTA tax may also be held liable for payment of the tax, as well as any applicable penalties and interest. However, even if the transferee fails to deduct, withhold and pay over the tax, the transferee will not be liable for such failure if the transferor's tax liability with respect to the transfer was satisfied by either (1) the transferor's filing of an income tax return, and payment of any tax due, with respect to the transfer or (2) the issuance of a withholding certificate by the service which establishes that no withholding is required.

The transferee's withholding of tax generally does not excuse a foreign person who has disposed of a USRPI pursuant to Section 897 from filing a United States tax return with respect to such disposition.

# Exceptions to General Rule

In general, the duty of a transferee to withhold under FIRPTA only arises when the transferor is a foreign person and the transferee is acquiring a USRPI. In addition, certain transactions are specifically expected from the FIRPTA withholding requirements.

# Transferor Not a Foreign Person

A transferor of a USRPTA is not subject to the FIRPTA withholding requirements if, prior to or at the time of the transfer, the transferor furnishes to the transferee an affidavit stating, under the penalty of perjury, that the transferor is not a foreign person, and setting forth the transferor's name, identifying number, and home or office address.

The transferee is required to retain this affidavit until the end of the fifth taxable year following the taxable year in which the transaction takes place. A transferee is not entitled to rely upon a transferor's affidavit if the transferee either has actual knowledge that the affidavit is false or receive notice from an agent of the transferee or transferor that such affidavit is false.

# Transferred Property Not a USRPI

No withholding is required where the transferee acquires only property that is not considered a USRPI. For example, no withholding is required upon the acquisition of an interest in a domestic corporation if any class of stock of the corporation is regularly traded on an established securities market.

Moreover, no withholding is required upon the acquisition of an interest in a domestic corporation if the transferor provides the transferee with a copy of a statement issued by the corporation which certifies that the corporation is not and has not been a USRPHC during the applicable period and that the transferred interest is not a USRPI.

## Certain Residential Transfers

The transferee also is not required to withhold FIRPTA tax from the transferor where the property is acquired for use by the transferee as a residence and the transferor's amount realized upon the disposition of such property does not exceed $300,000.

For these purposes a USRPI is acquired for use as a residence where on the date of the transfer the transferee has definite plans to reside at the property for at least 50% of the number of days that the property is used by any person during each of the first two twelve-month periods following the date of transfer. A transferee is considered to reside at a property on any day on which a member of the transferee's family resides at the property.

## Nonrecognition Transfers

A transferee is not required to withhold from his transferor if the transferor notifies the transferee that the transferor need not recognize gain on the transfer under a provision of the code or a United

States treaty and the transferee provides a copy of such notice to the service by the twentieth day after the date of the transfer together with a cover letter which sets forth certain information concerning the transferee.

However, a transferee must withhold if the transferor qualifies for nonrecognition treatment for only part of the gain realized or the transferee knows, or has reason to know, that the transferor is not entitled to the nonrecognition treatment so claimed. If the transferor claims nonrecognition on the sale or exchange of a principle residence in the United States has not been purchased as of the date of sale, then additional information must be provided by the transferor.

USRPI Acquired Pursuant to or in Lieu of Foreclosure. The FIRPTA withholding rules have a special application to a transferee that acquires a USRPI pursuant to a foreclosure or voluntary conveyance of a deed in lieu of foreclosure, under a mortgage, deed of trust or other security arrangement. A transferee that acquires a USRPI pursuant to a foreclosure must generally withhold a tax equal to 10% of the amount realized at the foreclosure sale; however, if the transferee complies with certain notice requirements, the transferee may be able to withhold a lesser amount.

A transferee that acquires a USRPI by voluntary conveyance of a deed in lieu of foreclosure must generally withhold a tax equal to 10% of the amount realized by the debtor/transferor. However, no withholding is required if:

1. The transferee is the only person with security interest in the property.
2. No cash or other property (other than incidental fees incurred with respect to the transfer) is paid, directly or indirectly, to any person with respect to the transfer.
3. Certain notice requirements are met.

In addition, no withholding is required under FIRPTA with respect to any amount realized by a grantor upon the grant or lapse of an option to acquire a USRPI. However, a transferee of an option to acquire a USRPI must deduct and withhold the 10% tax of the amount realized by the transferor upon the disposition. Furthermore, withholding is required on the amount paid for an option to purchase a USRPI upon the exercise of such option by its holder.

# Other Exceptions

No withholding of tax is required with respect to any acquisition of property by the United States, a state or possession of the United States, a political subdivision thereof, or the District of Columbia.

A foreign government which is the transferor of a USRPI is treated as a foreign person and is generally subject to tax under FIRPTA. Therefore, the transferee is required to withhold unless the foreign government furnishes the transferee with proper notice of nonrecognition treatment.

When a foreign government or international organization is the transferee of a USRPI, it is in turn subject to the FIRPTA withholding rules, and so is required to withhold tax upon acquisition of a USRPI from a foreign person.

## Limitations on and Adjustments to Amount Required to Be Withheld

### Bases for Issuance of Withholding Certificate

The service has issued regulations which explain the three situations in which, and the process by which, a withholding tax imposed on a foreign person's sale of a USRPI.

First, the service may issue a withholding entirely or permits a transferee to withhold an adjusted amount reflecting the transferor's maximum tax liability.

A transferor's maximum tax liability is equal to the sum of (1) the maximum amount of tax which could be imposed on that transferor with respect to the disposition of the subject USRPI plus (2) the amount of any unpaid withholding tax liability of the transferor pursuant to the acquisition of the subject USRPI or a predecessor interest.

Second, the service will issue a withholding certificate that excuses all withholding by the transferee if both (1) the transferor's gain from the disposition of the USRPI will be exempt from United States tax and (2) the transferor has no unsatisfied withholding liability. For purposes of this exception, a transferor's gain from the disposition of a USRPI will be considered exempt from United States tax under certain circumstances.

The transferor's being an integral part of a controlled entity of a foreign government is such a circumstance. Other such circumstance include disposition of the USRPI which does not constitute a commercial activity, or where the transferor is entitled to the benefits of an income tax treaty provides for such an exemption.

Third, the service will also issue a withholding certificate that excuses withholding entirely, or permits a transferee to withhold a reduced amount, if either the transferee or the transferor enters into an agreement for the payment of the FIRPTA tax with the service. This agreement must set forth, in detail, the rights and obligations of both the taxpayer and the service, and the taxpayer must provide the service with a security instrument or other acceptable form of security.

# Process for Obtaining Withholding Certificate

A withholding certificate may be obtained by filing an application with the service. Either a transferor or a transferee may apply for, and obtain, a withholding certificate. This application must be signed by the individual taxpayer, by a responsible officer in the case of a corporation, by a general partner in the case of a partnership, and by a trustee, executor or other fiduciary with like status in the case of a trust or estate. The service will act upon an application for a withholding certificate within ninety days of its receipt.

If the taxpayer receives a withholding certificate prior to the transfer, such certificate notifies the transferee that no withholding is required. If the withholding certificate is received after the transfer, such a certificate may serve as an authorization for a refund.

The service may also issue a blanket withholding certificate that excuses withholding with respect to multiple dispositions of USRPIs by the transferor during a period of no more than twelve months. A blanket withholding certificate may be issued if the transferor provides a letter of credit or a guarantee and enters into an agreement with service securing the payment of the tax with respect to the project dispositions covered by the certificate.

## Duties and Liabilities of Agents

The FIRPTA withholding rules do not require a transferee to withhold if the transferor furnishes an affidavit stating that the transferor is not a foreign person, and thus not subject to FIRPTA. However, the withholding rules prevent a transferee from avoiding withholding by using agents and subsequently claiming that he had no knowledge that the transferor's affidavit of nonforeign status was false.

Both the code and the regulations require that an agent must notify the transferee that the transferor's affidavit is false if the agent has actual knowledge of the falsity. An agent required to notify the transferee must do so in writing as soon as possible after learning of the false affidavit, so long as such notification occurs prior to the transferee's payment of consideration. If the agent will satisfy his duties by notifying the transferee within three days of the discovery. If the agent fails to notify the transferee, the agent then takes on the duty to deduct, withhold and pay over the required amount.

For purposes of FIRPTA withholding, an agent is defined to include any person who represents the transferor or transferee in any negotiation with another person or in the settlement of a transaction. An agent is also any person who represents or advises a corporation, partnership, trust, or estate with regard to a distribution of a USRPI.

However, settlement officers and clerical personnel are not agents if they are only connected to the transactions in minimal way.

An agent must provide notice to the transferee, or to the fiduciary of a transferee which is an entity, if the transferor has furnished to the transferee or its fiduciary an affidavit stating either (1) that the interest to be transferred is not a USRPI, and the agent knows that such statement is false, or (2) that the transferor is not a foreign person and either the agent has actual knowledge that such affidavit is false or the agent represents the foreign corporation that made such a certification.

An agent who fails to provide notice is held responsible for the tax that the transferee would have been required to withhold had such notice been given. However, the agent's liability is limited to the amount of compensations the agents derives from the transaction.

## Withholding on Distributions and Other Transactions by Corporations, Partnerships, Trusts, and Estates

FIRPTA provides special withholding rules which are applicable to specific transactions entered into by certain corporations, partnerships, trusts, and estates.

## Income Inclusions by Domestic Partnerships, Trusts, and Estates

In general, the code and regulations provide that if a domestic partnership, trust or estate disposes of a USRPI and any partner, beneficiary or owner of the entity is a foreign person, then the partnership, trustee or executor must withhold a tax equal to 34% of the gain realized on the disposition to the extent such gain is allocable to the foreign person's ownership. However, temporary regulations amending Regulation 1.1445-5(b) and (c), if and when adopted as final regulations, provide that a distribution by a partnership, trust or estate shall not be subject to withholding until the service otherwise provides in a later treasury decision under Section 897(9) of the code.

In addition, the temporary regulations provide that, until the service decides otherwise, no withholding is required with respect to the disposition of an interest in trust, estate or partnership that owns a USRPI, except in the case of a partnership in which 50% or more of the value of the gross assets consists of USRPIs, and 90% or more of the value of the gross assets consist of USRPIs plus any cash or cash equivalents. Notwithstanding these temporary regulations, existing regulations provide that a partnership must withhold a tax equal to 34% of each foreign partner's distributive share of the gain realized by the partnership upon the disposition of each USRPI. In the case of dispositions by trusts or estates, the trustee, fiduciary, executor or equivalent must (1) establish a USRPI account and enter into such account all gains or losses realized during the taxable year from disposition of USRPIs and (2) withhold a tax equal to 34% of any distribution to a foreign beneficiary that is attribute to the balance of the USRPI account on the day of the distribution.

Other exceptions to the general withholding rule provide that a domestic partnership, trust or estate is not required to withhold upon its distribution of a USRPI with respect to any partner or beneficiary that it determines not to be a foreign person. Similarly, no withholding is required if a domestic partnership, trust or estate determines that the property disposed of is not a USRPI or if the service issues a withholding certificate, which so provides.

Or if the service issues a withholding certificate which so provides. Finally, withholding is not required if the property is disposed of in a transaction where gain is not recognized due to a nonrecognition provision of the code or a United States treaty.

In the case of a partnership or a trust having more than one hundred partners or beneficiaries, the partnership or fiduciary of the trust may elect to be treated under an alternative withholding rule, provided the interests in the partnership or trust are not regularly traded on an established securities market.

Under this alternative rule, the partnership or trust must generally withhold from each distribution to a foreign person 34% to

the extent of that foreign partner's or foreign beneficiary's proportionate share of the current balance of the entity's Section 1445(e)
(1) account. The current balance of this account generally equals the
total amount of net gain realized by an entity from the transfer of
USRPIs, subsequent to the entity's election of this alternative rule,
less the total amount of all distributions by the entity to domestic
and foreign distributees from such account.

# Distributions of USRPIs by Foreign Corporations

A foreign corporation that distributes a USRPI must deduct
and withhold a tax equal to 34% of the amount of gain recognized
by it. Of course, no withholding is required where the property distributed is not a USRPI or where the service has issued a withholding
certificate that so provides.

# Distributions by USRPHCS to Foreign Shareholders

A domestic corporations which qualifies as USRPHC that distributes any property to a foreign person holding an interest in the
corporation may be required to deduct and withhold a tax equal to
10% of the fair market value of the property distributed to the foreign person. Such withholding obligation arises only if (1) the foreign person's interest in the corporation constitutes a USRPI and (2)
the property is distributed in a corporate liquidation or in partial
redemption of the corporation's stock.

No withholding is required in this context where the foreign
person's interest is not a USRPI, the distribution is accomplished
pursuant to a nonrecognition provision of the code or United States
treaty, the interest holder is not a foreign person, or an appropriate
withholding certificate has been issued by the service.

Withholding is also required where a USRPHC distributes a USRPI to a foreign person as a dividend. In general, the USRPHC must withhold from the foreign person tax equal to 30% of the amount of distribution.

# Rules of General Application

As discussed above, FIRPTA withholding in the context distributions and other transactions by the corporations, partnerships, trusts, and estates is subject to special rules which are designed to fit the particular circumstance. Within the scope of these special rules, certain guidelines and rules of general application nonetheless apply.

One guideline is that FIRPTA never requires double withholding. Thus, if a tax is required to be withheld under a special rule, then the transferee is not required to withhold additional tax pursuant to the general withholding rules of Section 1445(a).

In addition, FIRPTA withholding is not required under the special rules of Section 1445(e) where a nonrecognition provision of the code or a United States treaty applies, provided the entity, or fiduciary of the entity, properly notifies the service.

Generally, FIRPTA withholding is required only where a foreign person disposes of a USRPI; therefore, the FIRPTA withholding rules only apply to entities that transfer property where a holder of an interest in the entity is a foreign person.

The special FIRPTA withholding rules are not applicable where the property transferred by the entity is not a USRPI.

An entity, or a fiduciary of an entity, subject to the special withholding rules must generally report and pay over to the service any tax withheld by the twentieth day after the date of the transfer.

In addition, the withholding of tax by an entity, or fiduciary thereof, does not relieve a foreign person, otherwise subject to United States tax, from filing a United States tax return. Finally, the regulations permit the use of withholding certificates where the special rule of Section 1445(e) apply. These rules are substantially the same as the rules governing the use and availability of withholding certificates in regular context; therefore, a detailed discussion of this regulation is not provided.

## Withholding When Foreign Corporation Has Elected to Be Treated as Domestic Corporation

As discussed earlier, certain foreign corporations may elect to be treated as domestic corporations for FIRPTA tax purposes. When a foreign corporation has so elected, such corporation is generally treated as a domestic corporation for purposes of FIRPTA withholding. Therefore, dispositions of interests in electing foreign corporations are subject to the regular FIRPTA withholding rules. Thus, when a foreign person disposes of an interest in an electing foreign corporation, and the interest is a USRPI, the transferee is required to deduct, withhold and pay over as tax the amount required by the general withholding rule.

A foreign corporation that has elected to be treated as a domestic corporation may provide a transferee with a certification of non-foreign status in connection with the corporation's disposition of a USRPI.

Where a foreign corporation has made an election to be treated as a domestic corporation, the corporation is not required to withhold from a foreign person a tax upon the corporation's gain recognized from the distribution of a USRPI. However, an electing corporation is required to withhold with respect to the nondividend distribution of any property to an interest holder that is a foreign person where the interest in the electing corporation constitutes a USRPI.

# FIRPTA Reporting Requirements

Before payment of the FIRPTA tax was protected by the current withholding rules, payment of the tax was enforced through a system of information reporting designed to identify foreign owners of real property. This reporting scheme was complex and extensive. For example, different reporting requirements were imposed for domestic corporations having foreign persons who owned substantial real property interests but who were not engaged in a United States trade or business.

Final regulations as to the reporting rules were never issued because the Tax Reform Act of 1984, generally repealed the FIRPTA reporting scheme. Congress replaced the ineffective reporting system with the present withholding system because withholding is a means of collecting the FIRPTA tax and eliminates many of the problems inherent in a reporting system.

While the Tax Reform Act of 1984 generally repeals the prior FIRPTA reporting rules, it also authorizes the service to require reporting by foreign persons holding direct investments in USRPIs. A foreign person is considered to hold a direct investment in a USRPI if such person did not engage in a United States trade or business at any time during the calendar year and the fair market value of the USRPIs held directly by such person was $50,000 or more at any time during the calendar year.

The service has not yet provided regulations regarding the new FIRPTA reporting requirements.

## Penalties for Failure to Comply

A penalty is imposed on taxpayers failing to comply with the FIRPTA reporting requirements of Section 6039C. This penalty is generally equal to $25 per day for failure to file any return required by Section 6039C unless the taxpayer shows that such failure is due to reasonable cause and not willful neglect. However, for any such calendar year, such penalty can never exceed the lesser of $25,000 or 5% of the aggregate fair market values of the USRPIs held by the taxpayer during the calendar year.

Just as the current FIRPTA reporting requirements are not currently effective, the penalty for failing to report also is not currently in effect.

# Additional Taxes Imposed on Foreign Corporations Having Branch in United States—Introduction

This chapter has previously discussed the basic regimens under which foreign investors are taxed with respect to their operation of United States real estate, or real estate related, investments and the taxing and withholding provisions under FIRPTA. The following four sections discuss two additional taxes, the branch profits tax and the branch level interest tax, that were enacted by the Tax Reform Act of 1986, and apply to foreign corporations having taxable years beginning after December 31, 1986.

The branch profits tax is an additional tax imposed on so much of a foreign corporation's earning and profits, after certain adjustments, that are attributable to its income that is or treated as, effectively connected with United States trade or business. The branch profits tax was enacted to achieve a greater parity between the remittance to a foreign corporation of profits attributable to such corporation's income effectively connected with United States trade or business and the distribution of earnings to a foreign corporation that is engaged in the conduct of a United States trade or business through a United States subsidiary.

The branch level interest tax generally treats any interest paid by the United States trade or business of a foreign corporation as if it were paid by a domestic corporation for the purposes of taxing the recipient and for withholding purposes.

Also, to the extent a United States branch is allowed and interest deduction which is in excess of the amount of interest actually

HERMAN R. WILLIAMS

paid by it, then the foreign corporation itself will be taxable on such
excess in the same manner as if the excess were interest paid by the
foreign corporation by a wholly owned domestic corporation.

The following sections set forth the rules of the branch profits
tax and the branch level interest tax, and, in addition, discuss how
these taxes are affected by United States tax treaties.

## Branch Level Profits Tax

The branch profits tax is a 30% tax imposed on a foreign
corporation's "dividend equivalent amount." The dividend equivalent amount is intended to equal the foreign corporation's after-tax
United States earnings and profits that are not reinvested in the corporation's United States business. As such, the dividend equivalent
amount is similar to the net earnings of a United States subsidiary
of a foreign parent which would be available for distribution to the
parent company.

The branch profits tax attempts to achieve congress's goal of
obtaining greater parity in the tax treatment between the taxation
of a foreign corporation's United States earnings and the profits to
the.corporation and the taxation of distributions of a United States
subsidiary's profits to its foreign parent.

The dividend equivalent amount is equal to the foreign corporation's effectively connected earnings and profits for the calendar
taxable year, as adjusted for certain amounts. Note that the determination of the dividend equivalent amount begins with a foreign
corporation's effectively connected earnings and profits and not
the corporation's effectively connected taxable income, because the
branch profits tax is a tax on an amount which was hypothetically
distributed by a foreign corporations United States branch as a dividend. The earnings and profits concept is used in order to reflect
a corporation's dividend-paying ability. The foreign corporation's
effectively connected earnings and profits is adjusted so that such
amount does not include income from the operation of foreign regis-
tered ships or aircraft which are excluded from gross income, income
treated as effectively connected which relates to foreign trade income

of a foreign sales corporation, gain on the disposition of shares in a United States real property holding corporation, or income treated as effectively connected with the conduct of a trade or business which is related person insurance income.

Finally, a foreign corporation's dividend equivalent amount must be adjusted for changes in the corporation's United States net equity. The term "United States net equity" means a foreign corporation's United States assets reduced by its United States liabilities. Note that the terms "United States assets" and "United States liabilities" are defined to include only those assets and liabilities of the corporation that are connected with the conduct of the corporation's United States trade or business.

The dividend equivalent amount is reduced by the excess of the United States net equity of the foreign corporation at the close of its taxable year over its United States net equity as of the close of the preceding taxable year. The reduction is made because the increase hi the United States net equity year is presumed to be attribute to the investment of effectively connected funds which would otherwise have been available for a dividend payment.

In other words, an increase in United States net equity indicates that the profits generated by the corporation have not been remitted to the foreign home office. Conversely, the code requires that decreases in United States net equity from one taxable year to the next be added to a foreign corporation's dividend equivalent amount. Once the dividend equivalent amount is calculated, the 30% branch tax is imposed thereon.

To further the purpose of the branch profits tax, the service has issued temporary regulations providing general guidance with respect to the branch tax and, inter alia, that the branch profits tax will generally not be imposed on:

1. The complete termination of a foreign corporation's United States trade or business.
2. Certain liquidations or reorganizations of a foreign corporation that has conducted a United States trade or business.

3. A Section 351 incorporation of a foreign corporation's United States trade or business.

# Branch Level Interest Tax

Under prior law, interest paid by foreign corporations engaged in the conduct of a United States trade or business was generally not United States source income and such interest payments were generally not subject to United States withholding tax unless 50% of the foreign corporation's gross income was effectively connected with a United States trade or business.

The branch level interest tax generally provides that, in the case of a foreign corporation engaged in a United States trade or business (or having gross income treated as effectively connected with the conduct of a United States trade or business), any interest paid by such corporation's United States trade or business is treated, for the purposes of imposing a tax on the recipient and for withholding purposes, as if such interest were paid by a domestic corporation. This treatment generally causes such interest to be United States source income under Section 861 (a)(l); therefore; the payment of this interest is subject to withholding by the payor and taxation by the recipient. The general withholding rule applies unless the amount of tax is reduced, or eliminated, by either a specific code provision or a provision of a United States treaty.

"Interest paid by United States trade or business" is defined ad interest that is paid with respect to one of four classes of liabilities. The first class consists of liabilities identified as liabilities of a United States trade or business on the foreign corporation's books.

The remaining classes generally consist of liabilities that are treated as liabilities of a United States trade or business for regulatory or income tax purposes, liabilities that are predominantly secured by United States assets, or liabilities that give rise to certain nondeductible interest, such as capitalized interest which is related to United States assets.

The branch level interest tax also provides that to the extent the amount of interest allowable to a foreign corporation as a deduction under Section 882 in computing its effectively connected taxable income exceeds the interest actually paid by the United States branch, such excess is treated as if it were interest paid to the foreign corporation by a wholly owned domestic subsidiary on the last day of the foreign corporation's taxable year.

The effect of this provision is that the corporation itself will be taxable, and subject to withholding, on this excess amount. Temporary regulations permit a foreign corporation to elect to reduce its excess interest by the amount of interest paid by a United States trade or business in a different taxable year than the year in which the excess interest is paid. This election prevents the same interest payment from being included as both interest paid by a United States trade or business and excess interest.

## Interplay of Branch Level Taxes and United States Income Tax Treaties

In general, no foreign corporation is exempted from the branch profits tax or the branch level interest tax due to the existence of a tax treaty between the United States and foreign country unless such treaty is an income tax treaty and the foreign corporation is a "qualified resident" of such foreign country.

The amount of protection which a treaty will afford a foreign corporation is dependent upon whether the corporation is a qualified resident of the treaty country. In general, the term "qualified resident" for these purposes means any foreign corporation which is a treaty country unless either 50% or more, by value, of the corporation's stock is owned by individuals who are not residents of the treaty country, United States citizens or United States resident aliens, or 50% or greater of the corporation's income is used to satisfy debts to persons who are neither residents of the treaty country nor citizens or residents of the United States.

This definition of a qualified resident foreign corporation attempts to minimize treaty shopping, whereby nonresidents of the treaty country attempt to attain the benefits which the treaty accords corporations incorporated in the treaty country.

Exempted from the general percentage tests of qualified residency, and the considered qualified residents, are those foreign corporations which are residents of the treaty country if the shares of such corporation are either regularly traded on an established securities market in such foreign country or, if such foreign treaty country, the shares of the parent corporation are regularly traded on an established securities exchange in that country.

Also treated as a qualified resident is any foreign corporation which is a resident of a treaty country, is wholly owned (directly or indirectly) by a domestic corporation, and the stock of such domestic corporation is primarily and regularly traded on an established securities market in the United States.

The service also has the authority to treat a foreign corporation as a qualified resident of the treaty country if such corporation can satisfy the service that such characterization will not result in treaty shopping.

If a foreign corporation is a qualified resident of a foreign country with which the United States has an income tax treaty and such treaty allows for the branch tax, the rate of the branch profits tax is to be determined by the treaty. If such a branch profits tax rate is not specified within the treaty, then the permitted branch profits tax rate is that rate which the treaty specifies as applicable to the dividends paid by a wholly owned domestic corporation to its foreign parent corporation. In addition, all other limitations on the branch profits tax contained in the treaty are applicable.

A foreign corporation which is not a qualified resident of the treaty country, although such corporation is a resident of such country, will be subject to the branch profits tax even though exempt from income tax under a treaty business profits clause and even though the corporation would be entitled to nondiscriminatory treatment under the treaty.

In general, if a foreign corporation is subject to the branch profits tax, then no other tax or withholding obligation is imposed on any dividends paid by such corporation during the taxable year.

However, a foreign corporation may only obtain benefits of a treaty with respect to dividends which are received by such corporation, where the dividends are of the type described in Section 861 (a) (2)(8) if (1) such treaty is an income tax treaty between the United States and the foreign country of which the corporation is a resident and (2) such treaty and the foreign corporation is a qualified resident of such country.

The branch level interest tax is similarly effected by tax treaties. The code and temporary regulations generally provide that relief is available under the income tax treaty of a payor or recipient foreign corporation only if the foreign corporation is a qualified resident of the treaty country.

# LIFE IS ONLY A DAY

By Herman R. Williams

Life is only a day
Yesterday is but a dream
There is no tomorrow
There is only today
So don't rush it away

Life is what you make it
Death is how you take it
Love should be cherished by all mankind
Hate should be left far behind
Cherish each day as if it were your last
If bygones are cloudy, forget the past

Enjoy the earth surrounded by beauty
Kindness to others should be our duty
Lift up your heart and sing a song
For when your day is done, it will be gone

Don't sit around, worry, fret, and frown
For there is so much joy in our day to be found
Start your day with a hearty smile
And you will find it worth your while.

Be kind to all regardless of poverty or wealth
And pray their troubles will end and worries will melt.
Should God grant us another day
Let's start it off in the same gracious way.
Try to understand each person we meet

With a smile, a thank you, and a hearty greet
Try to lean just a little their way
Remember life is only a day.

Let's pray away all the hate we hear and see
From abroad and in our own backyard, the land of the free
Let's take all guns, bombs, and tuck them away
For remember, life is only a day.

When you start your day, and you feel a little blue
A prayer will help, regardless of what you do
Bend your knees and bow your head
Remember, God isn't dead.

# ABOUT THE AUTHOR

## HERMAN R. WILLIAMS

Few men possess a background that blends both the technical and practical aspects of real estate to equal that of Herman R. Williams.

As a practicing licensed real estate broker in Michigan, Canada, the Bahamas, Jamaica, West Indies, and the Island of Antigua, British West Indies, for over forty-five years, Mr. Williams has been actively engaged in all phases of real estate, including: sales, leasing, management, mortgaging, and appraising. Mr. Williams has owned, operated, and was president of his own real estate corporation, specializing in selling multimillion-dollar investment properties.

Mr. Williams has done feasibility studies for one of Toronto's (Canada) largest shopping centers. In addition to writing this book, Mr. Williams has lectured at the University of Michigan's Industrial Development Division. His topics covered the many foreign investments in the United States. Before entering the real estate business, Mr. Williams was party chief land surveyor for Clyde E. Williams and Associate engineering company in Freeport, Grand Bahamas, for many years.

Mr. Williams was one of ten top real estate senior sales representatives for Royal Trust Corporation of Canada and have won several awards for seven consecutive years.

While in real estate, Mr. Williams studied American Laws and Procedure, through a corresponding course, at LaSalle Extension University.

Civic affiliates include the following: former President, Northwest Business Council, Detroit, Michigan, and former Director, Mary Grove College Outreach Program, Detroit, Michigan.

Mr. Williams has visited many public schools, inspiring young people to have profound productive business and social lives.

*Mr. Williams is a devout Christian who is filled with the wisdom and the knowledge of God. It was through God's inspiration and encouragement that led Mr. Williams to write this book.*

www.ingramcontent.com/pod-product-compliance
Lightning Source LLC
Chambersburg PA
CBHW021417210526
45463CB00001B/421